T0038143

HOW WOULD YOU LIKE YOUR MAMMOTH?

HOW WOULD YOU LIKE YOUR MAMMOTH?

12,000 Years of Culinary History
in 50 Bite-Size Essays

UTA SEEBURG
Translated by Ayça Türkoğlu

THE EXPERIMENT
NEW YORK

How Would You Like Your Mammoth?: *12,000 Years of Culinary History in 50 Bite-Size Essays*
Copyright © 2023 by DuMont Buchverlag, Köln
Foreword copyright © 2024 by Max Miller
Translation copyright © 2024 by The Experiment, LLC

Originally published in Germany as *Wie isst man ein Mammut?: In 50 Gerichten durch die Geschichte der Menschheit* by DuMont Buchverlag, Köln, in 2023. First published in English in North America by The Experiment, LLC, in 2024.

The Experiment, LLC
220 East 23rd Street, Suite 600
New York, NY 10010-4658
theexperimentpublishing.com

THE EXPERIMENT and its colophon are registered trademarks of The Experiment, LLC. Many of the designations used by manufacturers and sellers to distinguish their products are claimed as trademarks. Where those designations appear in this book and The Experiment was aware of a trademark claim, the designations have been capitalized.

The Experiment's books are available at special discounts when purchased in bulk for premiums and sales promotions as well as for fund-raising or educational use. For details, contact us at info@theexperimentpublishing.com.

Library of Congress Cataloging-in-Publication Data

 Names: Seeburg, Uta, 1981- author.
Title: How would you like your mammoth? : 12,000 years of culinary history in 50 bite-size essays / Uta Seeburg ; translated by Ayça Türkoğlu.
Other titles: Wie isst man ein Mammut? English
Description: New York : The Experiment, 2024. | Includes bibliographical references.
Identifiers: LCCN 2024003610 (print) | LCCN 2024003611 (ebook) | ISBN 9781891011597 | ISBN 9781891011603 (ebook)
Subjects: LCSH: Food habits--History. | Gastronomy--History.
Classification: LCC GT2850 .S4313 2024 (print) | LCC GT2850 (ebook) | DDC 394.1/209--dc23/eng/20240226
LC record available at https://lccn.loc.gov/2024003610
LC ebook record available at https://lccn.loc.gov/2024003611

ISBN 978-1-891011-59-7
Ebook ISBN 978-1-891011-60-3

Cover and text design by Jack Dunnington
Translation by Ayça Türkoğlu

Manufactured in the United States of America

First printing May 2024
10 9 8 7 6 5 4 3 2 1

*For my parents—forever hungry for
knowledge, stories, and good food*

CONTENTS

"I hate history."

I hear this all the time—even from my own sister!—and when I ask why, the answer is invariably, "History is dry and unrelatable." After I tear my hair out in frustration, I take a deep breath and realize that it's not their fault but rather the fault of those teaching the history. Many of my own high school textbooks were, indeed, dry and unrelatable.

So why do I love history? Well, it's because I had great teachers who brought history to life through stories. For example, my American History teacher began our Civil War unit not with information about the political climate of the 1850s, as the curriculum recommended, but by reading a journal entry from William Bircher, a drummer boy in the Union army. William was the same age as we were, and his journal viscerally conveys the excitement and fear he felt going into battle—as well as the same teenage angst we were feeling in our own lives. Only once we were invested in the history did we ever crack open a textbook.

Now, when I ask myself how I can show a person who claims to hate history that it can be fascinating beyond all belief, my answer is food.

As far as I can tell, everybody eats—and more importantly, everybody always has eaten. When one looks at the mundane and relatable aspects of a historical figure's life, like their diet, it offers a gateway into history that even the staunchest history-hater can easily saunter through. This history-phobic person may find it hard to imagine themselves in the sandals of a gladiator prepared to die in an arena in ancient Rome, or in the boots of a weary soldier on the march in Napoleon's army—so instead, why not start with what those people may have eaten? Doing so sparks the imagination and immediately places them in that ancient arena or on the battlefield of Waterloo, and from there it's but a short journey to learning about other aspects of these historical lives. What did they think about? What did they do in certain situations? And perhaps most importantly of all, what were the consequences of those actions and how have they reverberated through time to affect us?

On my YouTube show, *Tasting History with Max Miller*, I introduce people to a historical dish and then surreptitiously deliver a fifteen-minute lecture about, for instance, how women eating pork in the Hawaiian islands led to the rise of Christianity and the eventual fall of the Hawaiian monarchy. By the time my lecture is done, the viewer has forgotten all about the food and is, instead, engrossed in the history. But without the food, without the bait, we never would have reached the history in the first place.

Fifty such pieces of historical bait are what Uta Seeburg has placed in *How Would You Like Your Mammoth?* She brings the characters of history to life in fifty snackable essays, all centered on the food eaten by people around the world and in varying social classes. Along the way, she sparks questions about how we live and eat to this day.

Now, if you already love history, then of course you're going to devour every word of this book, but if you're on the fence, or even if you detest history as dry and unrelatable, you'll quickly find yourself fascinated by the dining habits of sixteenth-century Catholics as you mull over what faux venison tastes like and wonder how in the world to make it. Each story is easily digestible (pun very much intended and meticulously thought through) and, like any good meal, leaves you wanting more. Maybe you'll hanker for just one more anecdote, or perhaps you'll be inspired to dive deeper into the topics she introduces, making these fifty stories the *amuse-bouche* to a historical smorgasbord.

M A X M I L L E R is the author of the *New York Times*–bestselling cookbook *Tasting History* and the creator and host of the viral YouTube series Tasting History with Max Miller, where he shares his passion for culinary history and historic dishes. Max's work has been covered in outlets including *America's Test Kitchen*, ABC's *Localish*, *Binging with Babish*, *Chowhound*, *Foodsided*, GLAAD, *KTLA Morning News*, Mythical Kitchen's podcast *A Hotdog Is a Sandwich*, *The Rachael Ray Show*, and Today.com. He's also a regular guest on Simon Majumdar's food history podcast *Eat My Globe*. Max currently resides in Los Angeles, California, with his husband, José, and their cat, Cersei.

GREETINGS FROM THE KITCHEN

I admit, I thought writing this book would be easy. It would, I hoped, serve as a culinary tour through human history, tasting spoon in hand if you will: peering into pots in Babylon, reclining around a table with the Romans, slurping a cure-all soup in the Middle Ages and—to finish—maybe sampling a deconstructed pea stew from a molecular kitchen. Each of these dishes is a child of its time, revealing something about the era in which it was eaten, how people moved from place to place, what was at the forefront of their minds—and what tasted good to them.

I soon realized that I'd have to travel farther than the cozy tour I'd initially planned. My spoon would be fishing about in some fairly dark recesses. Though food might seem like little more than one of humanity's essential needs, on closer inspection, the subject of food offers up a multifaceted menu of surprises. Food is social foundation and community, but it also harbors power and ruthless hierarchy. It's a jealously guarded national asset. The discussion around food is increasingly politicized—it can even be a catalyst for civil disobedience. The darkest chapters of human history are founded on the absence of food—famines—and were often paradoxically followed by periods of excessive feasting. Food is pleasure, of course, but it is also memory, escapism, and nostalgia. I encountered all these phenomena on my culinary journey, and now I'm pleased to unveil the buffet for your delight and delectation. I hope you're hungry!

Grilled Mammoth
North America

A kitchen requires two things: a heat source and tools for chopping and preparing food. But to cook a meal, you also need someone to acquire the ingredients. The astonishing success with which human beings developed is all thanks to a seemingly simple concept: cooking.

Humans were once unremarkable moochers who cowered behind bushes, hearts racing, while a pair of wild saber-tooth tigers tore a bison to shreds, and hyenas demolished the scraps. Only when the animals were finished would they scurry over to the well-gnawed bones and break them open with an axe in order to slurp out the marrow. (Cracking open bones and scraping out their contents might seem a little rough and archaic, but you can still find beautifully engraved silver marrow spoons, once ubiquitous in genteel Victorian manor houses, in numerous well-stocked antique shops; long and slim, they are perfect for reaching into the nooks and crannies of any bone.) And yet, it was these less than auspicious creatures who managed to cook their way to the top of the food chain. It's important to add that bone marrow is unusually high in protein, supporting the proper growth of the human brain. These growing mental capacities enabled humans to devise increasingly complex tools and ultimately led them to the idea of taming fire. And, voilà—a few hundred thousand years passed, and human beings were now capable of cooking, stewing, roasting, and smoking meat and vegetables, which, when raw, were hard to digest, less pleasant to eat, and sometimes even poisonous. (The concept of smoking foods may well have emerged after humans torched some forest or other and then gathered up the carcasses of a few animals boasting a particularly intense smoked flavor.)

And then, around twenty thousand years ago, the last Ice Age caused the sea in the region that would one day be known as the Bering Strait to freeze over so solidly that an adventurous set of human beings were able to cross it to reach the American continent. These people developed into extremely successful hunters, and it was likely their cavalier love of meat that drove the mammoth, the elk moose, and the ground moose to extinction. Their culture was given its name from the first location where their stone spear tips were found: Clovis, in modern-day New Mexico.

As well as the sheer physical necessity of eating, food has also always carried a social dimension, the core of which has changed from one era to the next. Sometimes, togetherness was paramount when people gathered around a table, while sometimes the food that was presented signified a person's social hierarchy. In some periods, the focus was all on the moment when the food was served, while another generation might suddenly take an interest chiefly in cooking for all those lovely little moments—sizzling melted butter, a steaming sauce boiling over, or basting a roast. The culinary minds of our Clovis big-game hunters may have revolved around a stage that comes somewhat earlier in the process, namely tracking and bringing down the animal itself.

Hunting a mammoth required planning, knowledge of the surrounding area, and plenty of patience. The Clovis hunters would typically seek out a hill by a river or water source where they had a good view and wait for a herd of mammoths to come to drink. While they waited, they would often occupy themselves by producing more lethal flint spear tips. These spear tips were relatively small, elongated, and razor sharp, with grooved bases. To pass the time, some of them would also scratch a decorative geometric pattern or a pretty flower onto a pebble. The spear tips would be attached to light throwing spears and hurled at the first unlucky mammoths that appeared.

The spear tips' grooves were a particularly advantageous feature because they immediately caused heavy bleeding in any animal, no matter where they struck. This meant that the hunter did not need to be a particularly brilliant shot; he would simply have to wait nearby until the mammoth grew so woozy from blood loss that he could get close enough to finish it off. The hunters would then cut up the colossal creatures at the kill site and carry them away, while the river ran a flaming red.

We can't say how the meat was ultimately prepared, or whether there were prized, delectable cuts—for instance, braised mammoth shoulder on a bed of wild herbs and fruits. How a mammoth of this kind tasted is another lost secret. For decades, a certain New York men's club claimed its members had dined on a piece of mammoth flesh, preserved in Arctic ice, in 1951, until unfortunately, subsequent DNA analysis proved that the diners at this Ice Age feast had merely eaten green sea turtle.

We can assume, however, that mammoth meat is rather tough, requiring long cooking. Perhaps it was a familiar evening scene for the Clovis people to sit around the fire, working away on their latest garments of mammoth hide and chatting about their day, accompanied by the wafting scent of slow-cooked mammoth, which soon got bellies rumbling. Until, eventually, someone asked the age-old question: *Is dinner ready yet?*

Grain Porridge and Einkorn Bread
Central Europe

For thousands of years, humans roamed forests and savannas, hunting and killing the abundant game and gathering and consuming the lush native plants that grew all around them. From time to time, a handful of wild-growing grains may have been included in that foraged mix, and the seeds would then be sown. It had grown warmer since the end of the last Ice Age. Cereal plants were shooting out of the ground everywhere and, gradually, humans began to harvest and process them, until eventually, they were cultivating them on a large scale. This was where humans used their competitive edge over animals, with whom they had to compete for easily accessible food: Human beings focused on foods like grains, which must be processed and cooked before they can be conjured into anything edible. With the advent of agriculture, temporary camps in dense meadows gave way to permanent settlements, villages with fields that were laid

out and tilled with ever more meticulous care and stren-
uous hard work from one generation to the next. "We did
not domesticate wheat," writes author and historian Yuval
Noah Harari, "it domesticated us."[1]

At this point in our history, the entirety of human existence revolved around food. A human being's everyday
life was defined by tending, cultivating, harvesting, and
processing it. Human homes were primarily constructed
to allow for storing and preparing food; barely more than
habitable storerooms with cooking stations. A typical
Neolithic settlement comprised several elongated houses,
which might border a small pond. The houses were quite
large, about sixty-five feet long, but each may have housed
as many as thirty people. This kind of house had a strong
frame made of wooden posts. Wooden rods interwoven by
tireless hands would be placed around the posts, and then
everything would be plastered over with rough clay. This
would be topped with a gabled roof thatched with reeds.
These roofs hung down almost to the ground, like floppy,
oversize hats. Sunlight would creep tentatively through
the open door at one end of the tunnel-like house.

Each of these houses had fire at its heart: the hearth.
The hearth was always in the middle, and the house's inhabitants most likely sat around it at mealtimes. The common saying that "the kitchen is the heart of the home"
has its origins here in the Neolithic period, the early days
of human habitation. Houses were also the driest places
in the village (and presumably the easiest places to keep
an eye on, should grain thieves start snooping around),

which is why there was at least one space for storing provisions. The open story under the roof offered storage space; there may well have been bunches of herbs hanging there to dry. Houses may also have been crammed with certain astonishing inventions that, alongside the cultivation of plants and settled life, were responsible for another major civilizing boost: clay pots. These pitchers, dishes, and amphorae were objects of great beauty. Curved lines, concentric droplets, and wave-like indentations were scratched into the fired clay; circles and spirals in earthy colors adorned the bowls' swollen bellies. Prior to the invention of these receptacles, foodstuffs were stored in holes in the ground and in baskets, where they either spoiled quickly or were eaten by all sorts of creatures. Clay pots ensured that provisions could be stored in large quantities for the first time. And, because they could be used to hold food and liquids over a fire, they made more advanced cooking possible.

Humanity's new existence as farmers did not really improve its quality of life. As far as their diet was concerned, by focusing on cultivated grains humans devoted themselves to a bland monotony that also carried a great risk. From this point onward, the human menu was distinctly more vegetarian; people were hunting less, and the age of keeping livestock close to home had begun. And so, from time to time, there would be meat from pigs, cows, sheep, or goats. (Animal domestication also had one unfortunate side effect: The animals brought humans into contact with a greater number of diseases.) Yet the most important food was wheat. Wheat was a massive gamble because, even though grains could now be stored, the stores would not last enough to balance out blighted harvests, which left an ever-looming threat of cruel famines.

On this day in history, however, the village is in a celebratory mood. The harvest has been a success and the stores are full. Wheat—in its very early forms known as einkorn and wild emmer, which have only just developed beyond their original, wild states—will be lightly roasted to make it more storable. Then comes the laborious process of grinding the wheat with heavy stones. A fist-size stone is rubbed over another that's larger and flatter and the monotonous, high-pitched knocking of the two colliding is a familiar sound of Neolithic daily life. After grinding, the husks (i.e., the shells of the individual grains) have to be removed—another thankless chore for which humanity can credit the agricultural revolution. Only then can it be made into bread. The bread, made from flour and water, is probably baked in a dome-shaped clay oven located outside of the house. Meanwhile, back at the hearth, a pot containing a kind of porridge is simmering over the open fire. Human beings will be eating grain stews such as these for a good while to come. The Neolithic version may have included cultivated peas or lentils as well as seasonal produce gathered from the forest. Wild fruits, mushrooms, and nuts might also have found their way into the hot pot in the heart of the house.

Soon, the bread is ready. Care has to be taken when biting into the freshly baked, hard, flat loaves; feeling a sudden sharp pain in the gums is not uncommon, as it is rare that all the husks would have been successfully removed. Mouths wounded by these tiny, hard, spiky husks were another bugbear of the Neolithic era.

The humans of this era lived for about thirty-five years on average before going to their graves. They worked hard all their lives and never ate particularly well. And yet, they were the very beginning of everything we are today.

Lamb Stew with Barley Cakes
Babylonia

One of the oldest written recipes in human history reads: "Lamb Stew. Meat is used. You prepare water. You add fine-grained salt, dried barley cakes, onions, Persian shallot, and milk. You crush and add leek and garlic."

These words in Akkadian Cuneiform were scored into a small clay tablet with a rush stylus around 1730 BCE, most likely in the city of Babylon. The unfired clay would have given way slightly under the fine tip of the stylus. These small, inscribed tablets were baked until hardened, turning a bright shade of orange. They were stored in archives, a kind of ancient, slumbering physical human memory that disappeared beneath earth and rubble, until they were excavated four thousand years later.

Other recipes were documented alongside this one: instructions on how to make broths, several stews, and a chicken pie that promised diners a surprise when the crust was pulled back to reveal the meat inside. In total, twenty-five recipes from this period were preserved and would go on to be deciphered in the distant future.

When the recipe for lamb stew was written down, Babylon was the largest city in the world. Its houses were huddled together, surrounded by a gigantic city wall. In the heart of the metropolis, strangers to the city would think they had strayed into a labyrinth, though the streets were ramrod straight. Yet the rows of houses looked confusingly alike, with smooth, windowless façades that concealed their interiors from outsiders' eyes. According to legend, in the center of the city, a tower loomed up, seemingly as high as the heavens, composed of numerous monumental terraces. The tower would have been even taller, but communication broke down when the people building it all suddenly began to speak different languages, leading to confusion.

What's certain, however, is that the rise of Babylon, one of the first major cities in the world, must have been shocking to experience. Perhaps writing, the most significant invention in human history, lies in this encounter with physical chaos, with the feeling of powerlessness resulting from a society growing at such an astounding rate. In Babylon and the other city states of Mesopotamia, which were themselves developing swiftly, the textualization of the world was meant to bring about order because how else would it be possible to get a grip on proud Babylon, this magnificent juggernaut, without governing it and creating structures captured in writing? Every detail of what made up this new, urban society had to be documented in order for it to be monitored. The invention of writing simultaneously heralded the birth of bureaucracy—and the first legal code. At first, scribes etched pictograms onto their clay tablets. A bowl stood for something like "food." A bowl with a head nearby denoted "eating." These pictograms were not just understood in terms of their direct description of an object; they were also read as sounds. Out of this, phonograms emerged, a practical and space-saving development. Writing could now represent the spoken word. It was a tremendous act of abstraction. It was in these phonograms that the Babylonian recipes were immortalized.

A large proportion of the Babylonians' preserved written records are lists. They list goods, public finances, the quantities of beer (brewed from fermented barley cakes) owed to laborers as payment, the number and proportions of city walls, ritual plinths, roads, and buildings in the city. In keeping with this, the first known recipes also read like simple lists of ingredients, although the quantities are not provided. The most important foods in the Mesopotamian region were barley, sesame, dates, and beer (in contrast to the Syrian-Levantine region, where wheat, olive oil, figs, and wine were the staples of choice). The Babylonians also began to take an interest in milk products, particularly different kinds of sheep's cheeses. Sheep were also processed for meat, and Mesopotamia's numerous marshland regions provided a variety of fish and birds. The Babylonians' lists also included around two hundred different types of bread baked from barley and wild emmer. Grains were still crushed and ground laboriously by hand using millstones, but thanks to the more complex hierarchies of urban societies, it was now possible to offload this thankless task onto prisoners.

Judging by the range and variety of ingredients, the lamb stew was probably intended for the tables of those in the upper classes of Babylonian society. It would have been prepared in a large pot over an open fire. First, the meat would have been fried in sheep tail fat. Water and milk would then be added little by little, along with various spices. The dish would be left to simmer slowly, and barley cakes would be crumbled into the stew to thicken it and add creaminess.

We can only speculate as to why these recipes were written down, despite the fact that they were probably familiar to everyone and had been passed on verbally for quite some time. The Babylonians' records clearly capture every aspect of their multifaceted daily lives— absolutely everything was to be recorded. The first tablet bearing a description of the city of Babylon provides another list of the dazzling facets of the ancient metropolis:

"Babylon—the seat of life!
Babylon—might of the heavens!
Babylon—city of truth and justice!
Babylon—city of abundance!
[. . .]
Babylon—its citizens are forever feasting!"

Here, we once again see an effort to gain control over such staggering abundance by fixing it in writing. Perhaps the recorded recipes are part of this strategy for imposing order. Add to this the fact that the written word means collectivization: Writing everything down and organizing it gave rise to a self-contained urban society. Consequently, these dishes were essentially declared to be common property. Food, as we will see, has immense power when it comes to forging identity. The lamb stew is distinctly reminiscent of Iraqi *pacha*, a dish that remains popular to this day, and that sees several cuts of mutton cooked and prepared in a manner similar to the way the clay tablets describe. So, you could tentatively describe the Babylonian stew as the first national dish, written down once and passed on for millennia.

Mummified Beef Ribs
Egypt

Picture a house full of nooks and crannies, dark, but pleasantly cool after the scorching heat outside. A deathly silence hangs in the air. It smells vaguely colorless, like sand and dust. The house comprises a long suite of rooms. Steep steps lead down to a basement with a long, tube-like corridor. At the end of this tunnel, you stumble down another flight of steps leading to a space reminiscent of a large storage cellar, stuffed full of objects, their outlines growing ever clearer as your eyes adjust to the gloom. Unexpectedly, beyond this peculiar repository, a large space almost like a hall opens up. Here, too, no space is wasted: There are precious ornately decorated chests, vessels, and statues wherever you look, sumptuous chairs adorned with gilded reliefs and hieroglyphs, as well as a couple of beds. At the center of this pile of treasures, which towers as high as the ceiling, are the coffins of the house's two inhabitants. We are in the burial chamber of

Yuya and Thuya, a married couple, and probably great-grandparents to the legendary Tutankhamun.

Somewhere among the mess of burial objects lies a small, oval sarcophagus. Inside is a miniature mummy, elongated and slightly bent: It consists of a couple of beef ribs, expertly mummified. Salts were used to remove any moisture from this once juicy piece of meat before it was carefully bandaged. The cloth used to wrap the ribs has been treated with Pistacia resin, an unfathomably expensive substance that would typically have been used to prepare only the mighty pharaohs for the afterlife. Clearly, someone wanted to make doubly sure that the tasty ribs would survive the long road through the Underworld.

For the ancient Egyptians, death was just the start of a new life, a kind of optimized version of one's previous earthly existence, and one that would ultimately last forever. However, the dead would have to withstand a dangerous journey and survive Osiris' strict death tribunal before access to the otherworldly blissful realm of Aaru would be granted. Those making the move to Eternity would bring with them everything they required for their own personal comfort. In most other religious traditions, it is generally assumed that entry to Paradise automatically guarantees beneficiaries an all-inclusive service, but the ancient Egyptians clearly harbored a certain mistrust in this idea and packed their graves full of whatever they thought would be needed for their final journey. Anything perishable—starting with their own bodies—had to be perfectly preserved in order to be taken into Eternity.

This was the reasoning behind the beef rib mummy. Some foods, like the ribs, lie in their own containers, which are fashioned into the appearance of the dish laid to rest: The burial chamber of Inenek-Inti of the Sixth Dynasty contained a sarcophagus in the shape of a roast goose.

Masses of provisions were laid on for every pharaoh throughout the rooms of their sprawling tombs. We know that Tutankhamun's tomb contained more than one hundred baskets filled with grains, loaves of bread, and fruits like sycamore figs, dates, melons, and grapes (though it is no longer possible to ascertain whether the fruit was dried first to make it last longer). The young departed ruler was also buried with a stash of honey and wine, as well as just under fifty wooden crates filled with mummified meat and poultry—including all kinds of small, delicate birds, ducks, and geese, though only the most luxurious of these were embalmed. It was the same for pieces of beef on the bone; it is quite clear that only the best, meatiest pieces were selected. You would be hard-pressed to find a piece of sinewy beef shank. Stewing meat was deemed unworthy of mummification, but a nice bit of tenderloin certainly made the cut. There was no fish, pork, or lamb to be found in the burial chambers, since these were all products common in mundane everyday meals in ancient Egypt. There was a definite hierarchy when it came to choosing foods for the afterlife; it was a matter of exclusivity as well as taste.

Poultry and beef were reserved for the elite, sizzling and spitting over an open fire or braised in pots. Cattle farming was an exclusive and expensive business, since most land was used to grow fruit and vegetables; rangeland was a rarity. However, the poorer population of ancient Egypt did not have too rough a deal: The Nile was full of fish and fruit, and vegetables thrived brilliantly in the warm climate. And across Egypt, fresh beer was brewed daily from barley, though workers could not afford wine. Wild emmer and einkorn grew in abundance in the fertile Nile region, so loaves baked with these grains and shaped into flat cakes were also a part of daily life in Egypt. After the laborious grinding process, the flour would be passed through a sieve made of rushes, though unfortunately, the mesh was so coarse that the little stones that had broken off the millstone would often find their way into the bread—yet another challenge to ancient Egyptian teeth, along with the painfully sharp husks that were rarely successfully eradicated from the flour. The bread, at least, was sweetened with honey, dates, and figs. Apart from the frustrating years when the Nile burst its banks and ruined the harvest, the ancient Egyptians could be forgiven for thinking they had found their way into paradise on Earth.

On festive occasions, the ancient Egyptians would place a cone made of propolis (bee resin) on their heads; to this day, we don't quite understand why, but it is possible that they were filled with perfumed oil that would produce a sumptuous, pleasant scent during the feast. The ancient Egyptians undeniably had a strong affinity for balsamic oils, even in life. Perhaps, as the scented oil dripped down their noses, they would picture with delight their future existence in Paradise, when their mummified geese would climb out of their roast-goose-shaped sarcophagi.

Only a small portion of the population was able to enjoy the same exquisite foods as the pharaohs, yet the delicacies of the few influenced the aspirations of the many. Juicy goose legs and delicious beef cutlets, preferably mixed with luxurious, delicately fragrant Pistacia resin—these foods were so desirable that people wanted to take them into the next life with them. In doing so, they hoped that they would eat like gods forever.

Mansaf
Syria

Few landscapes make a person feel as small as the desert does. Deserts are vast spaces filled with sand and dust, powdery mountains that give underfoot. There is no firm foundation as the ground runs with fine sand, drifting across the plains in waves. In amidst the sand are craggy, forbidding rocks. The nights are black with cold, while the days pass in a glare of heat.

The Bedouin have lived in these environments for millennia. They are nomads, moving between desert and steppe; they primarily farm livestock—goats, sheep, and camels—and throughout the year, they move from one grazing ground to the next, where they pitch their tents. Just under a thousand years before the Common Era, the Bedouin have already constructed a finely choreographed network of sites, settlements, and patterns of travel that follow the rhythm of the seasons and spread across the desert in present-day Jordan, Syria, Iraq, and

Saudi Arabia. Meanwhile, their most significant source of income derives from the elaborate logistics associated with growing trade routes: The Bedouin serve as desert guides for foreigners and their goods or impose a tax on unfamiliar caravans. Their diet includes a number of milk products, while meat is eaten more rarely. They also cultivate grains along their annual routes and use them to create the dough for thin flatbreads known as *shrak*, and to feed their livestock.

Bedouin society is composed of different tribes essentially allied to each other in friendship. Loyalties follow a strict hierarchy of family relationships: The more closely related you are to a person, the greater your fidelity to one another. However, there is another social virtue, a code, to which all Bedouins must adhere, and which organizes and maintains this entire societal structure: hospitality.

Hospitality is the most important principle for survival in the desert because it affirms that everyone has a duty to provide food and drink to any stranger who passes through. In this system, food is a vital source of nutrition but also a social glue and the foundation of community. *Mansaf* is a dish named after the large, round tray used to serve it that the Bedouins still prepare for their guests to this day. It has been served for festive occasions since time immemorial, made with a large proportion of meat to signify the host's generosity; the larger the mountain of meat, the more generous the host. First, the bread is baked. The dough is made of water and whole wheat flour and is spread paper-thin on a convex stone that has been heated for hours in the embers of a fire. The mansaf tray is positioned on a raised object and covered with the flatbreads. The meat, usually lamb, is cut into pieces and cooked in a large pot of water. Next to it is a smaller pot containing a large clump of melting camel butter. As the butter gently browns, it exudes a nutty aroma. When the lamb is completely tender, it is spread over the flatbreads, swiftly followed by the hot lamb stock, then the clarified butter; the entire process is repeated to create several layers.

Since the recipe for mansaf has predominantly been passed down orally, later being changed and adapted (these days, the lamb is cooked in fermented goat's yogurt and laid over a bed of rice; Jordan has declared this version its national dish), much of its earlier history has been forgotten. What seems certain, however, is that particular rites have been involved in its consumption for centuries. Before eating, all diners must wash their hands carefully. The dish is eaten standing up; the diners gather around the tray and must use only their right hand to eat, keeping their left hand behind their backs, so as not to place their unclean hand in the way of their neighbors. In addition to this, the host initially makes a point of standing to the side while his guests eat, generously offering one helping after another. In doing so, he signals the high regard in which he holds his guests—they must be tended to before the host can serve himself. When it comes to sharing a meal in Arab cultures, this order has persisted to this day, and it has become a natural reflex in other cultural circles too: *Guests come first.*

When Islam began to spread across the Arab world in the early seventh century, most adopted the new faith. Hospitality has remained a fundamental virtue in Islam; It is a holy law that goes beyond a culture of welcoming guests. Both the Qur'an and the Hadith go so far as to indicate multiple times that every Muslim has a duty to take travelers into their homes as guests and provide them with food and drink. The principle of sharing is rooted at the foundation of the recipes and communal food presentations that consequently developed. A meal in the Middle East is composed of several different dishes, served at the same time, for everyone to share. This stands in contrast to Western dining conventions, which developed in the centuries that followed and dictate that everyone is given their own plate, and several courses are served one after another.

Let's return to the Bedouins in the pre-Christian era. The meal of mansaf is enjoyed in the shade of a tent woven from goat's hair and it gradually comes to an end. The guests have kept to the hospitality customs and received their food and drink gratefully. In doing so, they have entered into a commitment to reciprocate their host's hospitality in the future. The host has therefore secured for himself a kind of insurance for his next journey through the unforgiving desert.

Food serves as currency in the desert's social security system. There is a contradiction inherent in hospitality; by giving strangers special treatment, you emphasize your own strangeness. This generates a distance amid an embrace. Thanks to his status as a guest, the stranger is given a fixed position in the group, which temporarily takes him into its midst. But while tucking into a piece of lamb dripping in nutty butter, and slowly slipping into a state of bliss, that sense of distance eases. The rule of hospitality establishes community—but it is the food that creates communality.

Grape Bread and Baked Onions
Etruria

It's a peaceful morning. The streets snooze in the sunlight; one lone horseman raises a little dust, which dances gently in the shimmering air before sinking to the ground again. The rider comes from the city-state of Rome, which has yet to become a location of great significance, and has just crossed the border into the neighboring state of Etruria. A land of green hills opens up before him. Across the landscape, plants grow and thrive, alternating between olive groves and wide meadows scattered with fruit trees and sheep—countless grazing, bleating white dots. Every hillside is littered with grapevines basking in the sun. The Roman rider comes across a local on horseback who returns his gaze with a friendly smile. He greets and addresses the Etruscan, but the Etruscan replies in a language that sounds stranger to the traveler's ears than anything he's heard before. He rides on, shaking his head.

We still don't know for sure where they came from, nor do we know where they disappeared to a mere seven hundred years later. Yet the Etruscans, who lived in the region of present-day Tuscany, Umbria, and Lazio between 800 and 90 BCE, were antiquity's richest, most vivacious, and most progressive gourmets. To the Romans they must have seemed like aliens, speaking a completely different language than their immediate neighbors. To this day, their language has yet to be fully deciphered. Their script, too, was like no other.

They were unusually skilled at extracting and processing the metal that could be found in plentiful supply in the gently rolling verdant region. Today, whole bronze Etruscan cutlery sets are steadily being unearthed, testaments to a culture of cooks and diners who put a lot of thought into using the fire to produce tasty food: carefully forged griddles and tripod stands, which made it easy to set a pot over the flames; portable clay ovens, which could be placed over the embers like oversize pot warmers. The heat would be concentrated and flow up to the cooking plates, which would already be laden with huge pots, perhaps containing a bubbling ragout of venison in red wine. There were intricately decorated bronze roasting spits in all sizes, and graters that looked suspiciously like the Parmesan graters we use today. There may have been a cheerful Etruscan lady asking, "How about a little cheese on top?" as far back as three thousand years ago. (According to ancient descriptions, she also would have been very beautiful and quite capable of holding her drink.) The Etruscans reputedly used these graters to finely grate chestnuts and beechnuts, but some sources interpret these theoretical cheese graters as proof that the Etruscans invented pasta—apparently, depictions of kitchen tools used for pasta-making have surfaced in some of their enormous, round burial tombs, which form whole cities of the dead (you couldn't possibly spend the whole afterlife unable to make spaghetti).

When it came to the rights of women, the Etruscans were far ahead of the Romans. Women played sport naked and feasted at the Etruscans' numerous banquets on an equal footing with men. Their Greek and Roman neighbors were appalled by this apparent immorality. "[Etruscan women] do not share their couches with their husbands but with the other men who happen to be present, and they propose toasts to anyone they choose," the Greek author Athenaeus complained.[2] This clearly didn't bother the Etruscans. Instead of reacting, they preferred to continue refining their cuisine.

None of their recipes have been successfully passed down, but some of their traditions have certainly lived on in Tuscan cuisine, and contemporary accounts suggest that Etruscan dishes were the soul food of antiquity. The most important ingredients in their dishes were olives, grapes, figs, pomegranates, and chestnuts, as well as chickpeas, lentils, and fava beans. They also grew and ate a variety of grains. In addition, this ancient cuisine was very strongly seasoned; the Etruscans favored a mix of sweet and very sour flavors (provided by honey and vinegar, respectively), and local herbs would then be used to add spice and, presumably, bitterness. They would bake whole onions in honey and red wine; take a delicious bite, like you would from an apple, and your mouth would fill with a hot, sweet-sour gush. To make red wine, grapes would be placed in a large stone basin and crushed underfoot. The freshly pressed juice, known as grape must, would then be stored in barrels, so any leaves, twigs, and little stones would sink to the bottom. Nothing else would be done to this proto-wine, which would be siphoned off and drunk directly—though not without first being mixed with water due to its considerable strength.

The Etruscans also enjoyed a moist, sweet bread made by kneading ricotta and crushed grapes into wholegrain flour and delicately scenting the soft, warm dough with cumin and aniseed. Meanwhile, a stew spiced to the absolute limit would be simmering away in the pot atop its bronze stand over the fire, and wild boar would be sizzling on the grill. The Etruscans kept cows, pigs, sheep, and chickens, but their favorites were the wild boar and deer that roamed the forests in plentiful supply, probably because their meat had a tangier, gamier flavor.

From 300 BCE onward, the Romans started harrying the free-living, hedonistic Etruscans and began capturing their towns, and by 90 BCE, Etruria finally became part of the Roman Empire. The people of Etruria were most likely scattered to the four winds; they were absorbed into the enormous, complex state of Rome, and their rich culture disappeared. Yet the memory of this earlier phase in human history remains—one in which women sat around the table alongside men; one with a smart, multifaceted system of agriculture; one with good, hearty cooking, and during which the pace of life was easy.

D. H. Lawrence wrote: "The things they did, in their easy centuries, are as natural and as easy as breathing. They leave the breast breathing freely and pleasantly, with a certain fullness of life. [. . .] And that is the true Etruscan quality: ease, naturalness, and an abundance of life, no need to force the mind or the soul in any direction."[3]

Sounds like a thoroughly bearable lightness of being.

Bread and Wine
Roman Palestine

The most momentous evening meal in the entire history of Christianity took place on a spring evening shortly before Passover in Roman-occupied Jerusalem. The traders herded out their lambs for sale, the bleating of which resounded through the narrow streets of the grand city in the mountains of Judaea. A great number of pilgrims, dusty and exhausted from their long journey, had already started haggling over the best specimens for sacrifice. In the morning, the lambs would be slaughtered in the great temple, its white marble glimmering over the roofs of the houses.

However, a group of thirteen men were already sitting down to an early Passover meal. The attention of those around the table was focused entirely on one Jesus of Nazareth, a wandering preacher. The high priest, who was in league with the Romans, wanted Jesus imprisoned because he feared he would incite the people to revolt.

After the group had started eating, Jesus looked around the table at his disciples who had gathered there. Their chatter died away. Jesus spoke calmly, saying, "Truly, I tell you, one of you will betray me." The others looked at him aghast, murmuring in consternation: Who could it be? Jesus had an answer ready: "The one who has dipped his hand into the bowl with me will betray me." At that point it was clear: It was Judas who had dunked his bread into the communal bowl at the same time as Jesus; he was the traitor.

In biblical times, the evening meal was served in a large dish placed in the middle of the table, and each diner would use their flatbread as a spoon to eat straight out of the dish. The Bible does not explain precisely which foods featured in the last supper, but it would most likely have included a simple vegetarian dish made of pulses, possibly lentils, simmered with onions, olive oil, and a little pomegranate juice. There must have also been roasted lamb on the table, to celebrate Passover. To prepare the Passover lamb, the animal's skin would first be removed and burned in the embers of the outdoor cooking pit. The lamb would then be speared on a long spit, lowered into the hot pit, and covered with earth until it was thoroughly well done. However, there are two things we can be sure of that were on the table that night: bread and wine.

Flatbread was ubiquitous in Roman Judea. Every day, women would grind grain using a hand mill comprising two millstones. The coarse flour would be sieved, mixed with water and salt, and kneaded to create a dough that would then be shaped into thin loaves. As day broke, the air would be filled with the scent of warm bread: The loaves would bake on hot stones in the embers of an earth pit or between the hot inner walls of brick-built communal ovens.

Wine was also commonplace. The poorer folk would mainly mix it with well water to cover the water's musty flavor—and for hygiene reasons, too. People had yet to discover that it was possible to sterilize water by boiling it.

After Jesus identified the man who would betray him and made it clear that he knew his death was at hand, he broke a loaf of bread into pieces and distributed it among his disciples before handing around a cup of wine. He then did something altogether unusual. He said, "Take and eat; this is my body." And as the cup of wine passed between the disciples, he explained that the wine was his blood. Though this might seem peculiar, perhaps even unappetizing, it marked the beginning of a ritual that would be observed for centuries. The last supper, shared by Jesus and his disciples, would be a holy meal.

At this time in history, it was nothing new for certain meals to carry religious significance. At the Seder, the ritual dinner held on the first night of Passover, the table was laden with purely symbolic ingredients: unleavened bread representing the flight of the Jews from Egypt (they'd had to leave in such a hurry that the dough for their bread did not have time to rise); salt water symbolizing the tears that were shed; various bitter herbs representing the bitterness of the slavery endured by the Jews in Egypt. And so on and so forth; everything that was eaten served to remind and unite those gathered at the table.

The Christian tradition, which Jesus founded on that spring evening, goes one step further: Bread and wine do not simply recall the last meal before he was martyred, but they ensure that, time and again, he takes up a seat among believers, becoming part of the congregation as they ritually eat of his body, incorporating it into their own. It is perhaps no coincidence that this most significant Christian ritual is a communal meal; few things harbor greater power to foment community.

To this day, bread and wine also remind us of the Mediterranean origins of Christianity, which emerged in a part of the world where fields and hills were abundant in grain and wine. The fact that Jesus lent such symbolic power to these two everyday foods tells us one thing above all: The Son of God did not come to sit among the elite. On the contrary, he would take up his seat among the very poorest.

Gladiator Stew
Roman Empire

It's a warm summer's evening in ancient Rome. The streets between the high blocks of houses are filled with noise that muddles the senses. Hordes of hurrying pedestrians push and shove. Farther ahead there are several ox carts blocking the path. Among them are horses, snorting, driven through the crowds by men in fine togas who don't give a thought for what damage they might do. Now and again corridors form to make space for a sedan in which a senator sits, huffing and puffing. The ordinary citizens groan as they press their backs against the brick walls lining the streets. All of Rome is in a hurry. It's time for the evening meal: the *cena*.

A babble of plebeian voices can already be heard echoing from the taverns where wine, olives, and bread are being served. The residents of the multistory *insulae* who prefer a hot meal turn to one of the numerous *thermopolia*, because the high fire risk means it is forbidden to light a fire in these rented houses. Cooking pots are set into the walled counters of these fast-food restaurants, their contents kept warm by a steady fire. There is bread and *puls*, a spelt porridge similar to polenta but with a tarter flavor. These are accompanied by vegetables, onions, garlic, cheese, and fruit, and sometimes a little cooked meat—and many herbs, which simmer slowly in the cooking pots and fill the space with their intense aromas. In these eateries, people sit on chairs—just one of the many reasons why members of the Roman upper classes would never set foot in such a locale, as only a dining couch would befit their rank.

The elite generally kept to themselves when it came to eating. For the Roman bourgeoisie, it was part of everyday life to host a convivial feast at home, where they enjoyed conversation and wholesome and tasty food. The villas of the richest and most important families in Rome saw their inhabitants sit down to the table full of anticipation, because it was there that unimaginably exclusive culinary creations would be laid on. Yet the creativity with which these dishes were prepared was not infrequently testament to an unprecedented kind of sadism: A popular trick involved having an animal fly out of one of the dishes, surprising the diners. Accounts speak of live thrushes sewn into the stomach cavity of a wild boar, flying out and up to the ceiling in alarm when the roast is carved. Even more sensationally, little birds might have been concealed in "piglets" made of cake batter, suckling at the teats of a slain wild sow. For later courses, the kitchen slaves might have present stuffed dormice, flamingo tongues, and spicy nightingale's liver.

Something had already manifested in this ancient society, something that would endure throughout the centuries that followed: Food now served to provide social cachet. What each social group ate was just as immutably defined as each Roman's position in the social hierarchy.

This was particularly clear in a small class of the population that found itself ranking lower even than slaves. Members of this group were at once idolized, enjoying a kind of glittering fame, and also despised, given an unflattering nickname in reference to the only food they really ate: *hordearii*, barley eaters. We're talking, of course, about gladiators. These professional combatants, who fought for their lives in the arena with swords, daggers, and throw nets, were strict, if unwilling, vegetarians— meat was simply too expensive for people of their ilk. Gladiators almost exclusively ate barley, beans, and pulses, sometimes mashed and sometimes as soup.

After a hard day's training in the practice arenas at the gladiator school drew to a close, the last sweaty fighter would stagger out. While the gladiators were massaged, the barley soup simmered in huge pots over fires in the school's kitchen. The first dishes of stew were served: a hot, creamy mass of overcooked pulses. The men took spoonfuls and winced a little, tears pricking their eyes: Ancient Roman cuisine typically used a mix of very spicy and contrasting flavors that hit the tastebuds all at once. Fresh rue leaves are almost unbearably bitter, but the Romans loved this herb and used it in almost everything. They were equally partial to pungent lovage and salty *garum*, a fish sauce made by mixing fish along with its innards with salt and leaving it to ferment in open pitchers in the blazing sun for three months. The stench was so strong that people were forbidden from making it in the inner cities. Yet, for the Romans (and the Greeks before them), the liquid that was produced and decanted into little bottles was an indispensable feature of their culinary arsenal. Its salty flavor was so intense that it made your whole tongue itch. These bitter, tangy, and salty tastes would once have been accompanied by the flavor of laser, a juice made from the Libyan silphium plant. It probably tasted similar to garlic, but sharper. (This herb died out in Nero's time; the ruler was said to have eaten the last remaining plant himself.) The lentils and chickpeas would have been cooked in water from the cisterns, so the entire dish would have taken on a slightly brackish bouquet.

There was a big advantage to this multi-faceted spicy flavor. It could be used to almost completely cover the unpleasant taste of certain foods—like the meat of the common crane, which tasted like rotten eggs. As well as manipulating the flavor, savvy cooks would add the element of optical illusion with increasingly sophisticated techniques for culinary trickery: Pork was presented as poultry, sows' udders as fish, and dog meat could be dressed up to look like hare.

But let's return to the gladiators and their barley stew. In the second century, the physician Galen of Pergamon hypothesized that the gladiators' diet might be responsible for a beneficial, though unintentional, side effect: making them fat and flabby. Professional fighters often cut somewhat chubby figures, and the additional body fat served to protect the organs if they received stab wounds. Nevertheless, according to contemporary analysis, gladiators' bone density was equivalent to that of competitive athletes; their bones were noticeably higher in strontium than the rest of the population. This may also be down to a special calcium-rich drink made of vinegar and vegetable ash, which was served after fight training. This was another form of nutrition reserved exclusively for one social group, and its distinctive power penetrated deep into their bones.

Injera
Aksumite Empire

There's a hiss of steam as the first drops of runny batter hit the hot clay plate. The round disc sits on top of a clay oven with a fire flickering inside. With a steady hand, a young woman pours out the batter in a large spiral, starting in the center and working outward until the whole surface of the plate is covered, by which time the batter is cooked through. Time blurs in this circular motion. Her mother used to pour the batter over the glowing hot plate just like this, and so did her ancestors before her; no one remembers exactly when it started. Made mainly of teff flour, this thin flatbread is known as injera. People have been harvesting teff here for millennia. Teff grows on the plains of the Ethiopian uplands as a soft, tall grass; it moves in the wind like the fur of a sleeping animal.

In the centuries to come, people will find the plates known as *mitads*, which once steamed over clay hearths, in Aksum, the capital city of the mighty Aksumite

Empire. In Aksum, huge stone slabs towered above the kings' tombs in the sultry air. These behemoths were stylized houses looming upward with a ludicrous number of floors and windows—testaments to the improbable, wild visions of the people who built them.

Injera batter is made from milled teff and water. The mixture is left to stand and ferment for a couple of days as the natural yeasts present in the teff seeds get to work. Every Ethiopian home has a corner filled with numerous covered containers full of fermenting batter and a dark, sour liquid that floats above the teff. It requires experience and intuition to know exactly when the contents are ready.

Next the batter is poured out onto the hot *mitad*, and as the injera cooks, an intense aroma rises from the hot plate. Countless pores and tiny craters develop on the surface of the flat, pancake-like bread; the texture of good injera is reminiscent of a sponge. The more tiny hollows the bread contains, the better it will be able to soak up the pastes, ragouts, and stews, known as *wat*, which are served on top. The soft flat bread, the size of a round tray, serves as both a plate and cutlery.

Next, individual palm-size portions of wat are distributed on top of the bread. There are many varieties of wat; *doro wat* contains chicken and boiled eggs; there is another variety with lentils; some with beef, goat, or lamb; and purely vegetable-based stews. They are all thick and compact, products of intense heat and considered slowness. First, onions are warmed in a dry pan until most of their liquid has evaporated. Then it's time to add *niter kibbeh*, spiced clarified butter, its nutty flavor blending with its aromatic spices such as cumin, turmeric, cinnamon, or *besobela*, Ethiopian basil, that add fragrance and depth of flavor. The onions are sweated on high heat and showered with herbs and spices until everything breaks down and becomes a thick mush, which gives the remaining ingredients their dense consistency.

Wat can be mild, spicy, or very hot. (Since the introduction of chile peppers to Africa in the sixteenth century, a blend of chile, coriander, garlic, ginger, and wild Ethiopian herbs has been used to create a pungent spice mix.) Each portion of wat on the injera is a different color and different flavor. Everything is brought together by the mildly sour taste of the soft bread, which is torn into strips by hand. Diners roll each strip around a dollop of wat before putting it in their mouths.

In the Aksumite kingdom of late antiquity, a group of people has gathered around the dish on the table. These are not just family members but neighbors, friends, and guests. Enjoying a meal together is one of Ethiopia's social foundations. Included in this is a ritual known as *gursha*: Everyone at the table readies an especially tasty bite—and then feeds it to their neighbor. There is a definite hierarchy to the order in which the gursha is carried out. The eldest and most important guests at the table are generally fed first as a mark of respect. Anyone who feeds a morsel to someone else can expect to receive a mouthful in return. And three portions per person are plenty: *One gursha makes enemies, two pulls them apart, and three brings them together,* as they say in these parts.

Feeding one another expresses care and devotion—it brings the element of cooperation inherent in the act of sharing food to the surface. In other cultures, however, it crosses the limits of acceptable table manners: Feeding may be considered intrusive, and from a certain age it may denote incapacitation and a loss of control. In the eyes of modern Western society, the mere act of eating with your hands, and not using sterile cutlery, may be a source of unease. This renunciation of trusted cultural tools that always serve to create distance between the food and the diner feels all the more outrageous the moment one is fed, simply, plainly, by a stranger's hand.

The Portuguese Jesuit Jerónimo Lobo described this practice in a flatly disparaging tone in the seventeenth century: "Everything they eat smells strong and swims with butter. They make no use of either linen or plates. The persons of rank never touch what they eat, but have their meat cut by their pages, and put into their mouths."[4] The French traveler Emilius Albert de Cosson was no less disconcerted in the late nineteenth century: "The bread was in large wafers, about as thick as a pancake, and a foot and a half in diameter. [. . .] If the Ras saw any of the native guests he wished especially to honor, he broke off a piece of the bread, rubbed it in all the sauces and rammed it into their mouths with his own hands." Yet he's willing to concede something: "They however managed to handle their food with such skill that very little mess was made in eating it, and though the bread was rather bitter, some of the sauces were good, and the meal was not so unpalatable as might be supposed."[5]

It's unusual that neither of these two Europeans seemed to spot the most obvious connection between these two cultures—Ethiopia was broadly Christian from the fourth century onward, and since the sixth century in the Christian church, it has been the role of the priest to place the bread straight into the mouths of the congregation during the Eucharist. However, there is an arguable difference between a religious ritual and a gesture performed as part of an earthly banquet (not to mention Western feelings of superiority toward Africa). The subject of food once again becomes a space in which intimacy and touch, distance and strangeness, are debated.

Cure-All Soup
Holy Roman Empire

Numerous fundamental meanings were ascribed to food in medieval Europe. The social act of eating together could be as binding as a contract. Ostentatiously seasoned and spiced food stood for wealth and power. On fast days, eating was subject to strict rules, which also made it an expression of a person's deep faith. The Middle Ages witnessed terrible hunger and spectacular feasting. And food was said to have healing properties.

As early as 500 CE, the Greek physician Anthimus wrote of the Franks' favorite dish, which was also used as a cure-all. Its primary ingredient? Raw bacon. Anthimus explains:

> Bacon fat which is poured over some foods and vegetables [. . .] is not harmful. But frying brings absolutely no benefit. As for raw bacon which, so I hear, the Franks have a habit of eating, I am full of curiosity regarding the person

who showed them such a medicine as to obviate the need for other medicines. They eat it raw, because it is very beneficial and as a remedy is responsible for their health. Its effect is akin to that of a good medicine for their internal organs, and if they have any difficulties with their bowels or intestines, it cures them. [. . .] Thick bacon, placed for a long time on all wounds, be they external or internal or caused by a blow, both cleanses any putrefaction and aids healing.[6]

In the Middle Ages, it was also popular for sophisticated tables to have some sweet confectionery to nibble on alongside lavishly spiced dishes—for health reasons. These small sweets were made from fruit, spices, and sugar. The last of these was thought to cleanse the body, benefit the kidneys, and neutralize harmful properties in other foods—sugar was seen as the sweet antidote to harmful gluttony. Sugar was even used to care for the teeth and remove greasy food residues. Monks liked to distribute gingerbread among the needy as a potent remedy.

Much of what we claimed to know about the body and nutrition throughout this time was based on the theory of the four humors, which originated in antiquity. According to humorism, the human body was composed of four fluids: blood, phlegm, black bile, and yellow bile. These bodily fluids were either warm or cold, dry or moist. Foods were also classified according to these properties: hot and dry, hot and moist, cold and dry, or cold and moist. Sugar was hot and moist, making it a good foodstuff because a healthy person's fluids were characterized by moderate heat and moisture. To help a patient's fluids achieve equilibrium, doctors would prescribe the relevant diet to iron out any imbalances within the bodily fluids. A bacon and sugar diet would certainly not have been out of the question.

However, medieval cuisine was fed primarily by knowledge about the healing properties of herbs and spices. There was a spiritual element to this knowledge. This subject takes us straight to Hildegard von Bingen, the twelfth century herbalist often held up as a saint, who lived and worked as a nun and mystic and wrote a number of pertinent texts in this field. Her influence has persisted over the centuries and still resonates in esoteric medicines and illustriously named herbal tea blends.

One of the results of her teachings was a certain wondrous soup regarded as a cure-all offering a firework display of fantastical effects. Here's how you make it: Gently cook down a handful of spelt with some soup vegetables: celery, fennel, and carrots. Now add the most important ingredients of all: basil, galangal, parsley, Bertram (a flowering plant in the daisy family), dill, and perhaps a bit of wild thyme.

According to Hildegard, basil is a cold plant that can help combat fever. (People who fall spontaneously mute are also advised to place a basil leaf under their paralyzed tongues to prompt their speech to return.) Galangal, on the other hand, is warm and medicinal and helps those suffering from a weak heart. Parsley eases a mild fever, but those using this herb are advised to exercise caution so as not to slip into melancholy because, Hildegard writes, "It begets solemnity in a person's mind."[7] The same warning also applies to the dill in the soup. To combat this, the reader is advised to take the precaution of adding Bertram to the soup, which should help clear the mind again. It also increases the quantity of good blood, cleanses the bodily fluids, strengthens the body's defenses and eyesight. Wild thyme, meanwhile, cleanses and heals the body from the inside out and, interestingly, is a remedy for scabies.

Few epochs were as strongly permeated by a belief in wonder and magic as the Middle Ages. Miracles from God, the enduring fear of hell and the devil, the power of talismans, gemstones, and amulets, as well as healers, soothsayers, spirits, witches, the power of herbs and foods of different temperatures, all of which bordered on magic, fit seamlessly into this profoundly mystical attitude to life. We can't really describe this as alternative medicine— medically speaking, at the time, there were few options beyond the application of select herbs and spices. And so, soups, sweets, and bacon were infused with a kind of everyday magic that could quickly turn miraculous. At no time has food been more spiritual, more wondrous, or more magical than it was in the Middle Ages.

Hotpot
Chinese Empire (Song Dynasty)

The two were neighbors, but they couldn't have been more different. On the one side was China, which, circa 1200 CE, was the most highly developed civilization in the world. It had a rapidly growing economy, prosperous citizens who loved expensive clothes and furniture, and an elaborate cuisine. It was a cradle of spectacularly beautiful art and fine literature. Printing was flourishing, with richly stocked libraries and excellent schools. The imperial manufactories were humming with activity across the land, and the nation had a rich understanding of medicine and science.

On the other side was Mongolia, inhabited by a nomadic, illiterate people who lived in felt tents. These people owned only as much as they could buckle onto a horse's back. They ate almost exclusively mutton and cheese, sewed their clothing from furs and hides, and unceremoniously burned their animals' dung to heat their yurts. Yet, it was these seemingly rough journeymen who introduced the Chinese to their national dish: hotpot.

Despite all their technological advantages, the Chinese people of the Song Dynasty had no real army to speak of. Due to a constant fear of military coups, the ruling powers forwent installing a serious military force and exalted the virtues of pacifism instead. Much to their misfortune, however, their coarser neighbors were brilliant warriors and excellent horsemen, who could fire lethal arrows over long distances using bows they made themselves, all while galloping on horseback. An even greater misfortune to befall the Chinese was the fact that a certain Genghis Khan had united the notoriously in-fighting Mongols, and dared to make a serious attack on China.

His grandson, Kublai Khan, ultimately conquered China in a nightmarish sea battle in the Bay of Yamen. The Mongolian fleet was laughably small compared to the Chinese one, but the erstwhile nomads once again proved themselves clever and bold. A thousand Chinese junks went up in flames, including those in which the women and civilians of the Chinese court had attempted to flee the battle; women tied weights to their waists and jumped into the water so as not to fall into the hands of the Mongols. The seven-year-old emperor and the last members of his dynasty also met their ends in the ocean's black depths. One of the proudest nations on Earth had been overthrown.

But after China's resurgence, in a tradition that continues to this day, its people would gather at round tables, around the same hotpot that their scorned occupiers first brought with them from their homes on the endless steppes. Human beings display a remarkable ambivalence in their relationship to food.

According to legend, the Mongols initially used their helmets as improvised cooking pots. They used them to heat broth over the fire and they would then poach small pieces of mutton in the stock. As for the story of the helmets, we will probably never know for sure if it's true, though it is plausible; soldiers have used their helmets for cooking throughout history. The fact is, however, that the Mongols brought their penchant for mutton to Northern China, where it remains one of many possible ingredients for poaching in a hotpot to this day. And it's certainly conceivable that the Mongolian nomads poached their meat in these mobile "pots," which also served as a pleasant source of heat to gather around on cold nights. Thus, in a way hotpot is not all that different from fondue. (The Mongols still practice a method for cooking meat without cookware; an animal will be slit open from top to bottom, and then the bones, meat, and innards are carefully removed. The meat, liver, and kidneys will be placed back inside the animal along with hot stones, and the meat will then be grilled inside the skin. The pleasantly warm stones, glistening with fat, are handed around before the meal begins.)

Hotpot spread quickly in China, mainly in the form of a pot with a kind of chamber in the center, which was filled with glowing coals or wood. Each region would go on to develop its own version of the hotpot. In the South, people prefer the broth to be sweeter; in the North, they prefer it salty. In the East, there's a preference for sour notes, while in the West, the broth is hot and spicy. The hotpot from the Szechuan region, famed for its peppercorns, is especially popular in China. The pot's steaming contents gleam bright red, while swollen peppercorns, chile peppers, and a whole host of spices float on the surface of the broth.

Hotpot gets to what is perhaps the most important element of eating: community. (Anyone these days who happens upon the bizarre idea of visiting a Chinese hotpot restaurant alone might soon find themselves sharing a table with an oversize cuddly toy, thoughtfully set aside for eccentric solo diners.) The pot will ideally be placed at the center of a round table, where it represents harmony and communion. These days, many hotpots feature two compartments rather than a central chimney: one containing a spicy broth, the other containing a milder one. The two compartments are curved like yin and yang and, together, create a whole. Diners place seafood, meat, and vegetables in the broth, and there may be a couple of *jiaozi*—dumplings—floating in the pot, too. They then use ladles, chopsticks, and skewers to fish their morsels from the pot while the windows around them steam up and the bustle of the streets outside disappears as if behind a curtain at the theater. At the end of the meal, the broth, rich and spicy from all the ingredients that have been dunked into it for hours, is decanted into bowls that are promptly drunk by the satiated diners with an air of reverence.

Counterintuitively, when Kublai Khan seized control of China, rather than seeking to impose Mongol culture, the Mongol ruler sought to become as Chinese as possible. He had Confucian and Buddhist temples built, as well as a palace city in the Chinese style. His eldest son studied Chinese literature and philosophy. And he would lay on lavish banquets far removed from his past life as a simple nomad. Despite this, the Chinese people were systematically suppressed. And in Khan's sumptuous palace gardens, you might encounter a yurt or two, where some of his followers still preferred to sleep. The Mongolian Yuan Dynasty remained foreign in China, swiftly declining following the death of Kublai Khan.

And so, after roughly one hundred years, the Mongols disappeared from China once more—but they left their hotpots behind. In China, sitting together around a hotpot became a culinary tradition that would endure much longer than the Mongol occupation.

Blamensir
Holy Roman Empire

When thinking about food, it's important not to forget about hunger. Hunger, in all its wild, merciless brutality, was a constant companion for people living in Europe in the Middle Ages. Even wealthy citizens witnessed famines; no one could control the seasons. Every harvest ran the risk of blight and livestock could always fall sick.

But during those times when the harvest was plentiful and the livestock fat, people responded to the never-too-distant memory of starvation with unrestrained feasting. Long dining tables would groan under mountains of meat, bread, and seasonal vegetables and fruit, everything prepared simply and without any appreciable culinary tricks. The happy eaters would huddle around the table: Communal feasting was also a mainstay of social life in the Middle Ages. In the Early Middle Ages, eating together signified an especially deep bond.

Sharing an evening meal with a business partner was akin to signing a contract.

In the High and Late Middle Ages, preparing food developed into an art as much as a craft. In the German-speaking world, an unknown writer first captured recipes in writing around 1350 CE, in *Das buoch von guoter spise*, or *The Book of Good Food*. At the same time, this concept of "good food" coincided with a widening social gap. Of course, there were differences between the food of the rich and poor during the Early Middle Ages, but these generally manifested in the height of the mountain of meat and the mass of stew. By the High Middle Ages, however, a peasant woman would eat her grain porridge and sometimes meat, its slightly coarse flavor masked by local herbs, while lords and ladies were served game, imported fish such as pike or cod preserved in salt, and poultry.

Poultry was especially prestigious because the higher from the earth a food was "harvested," the more valuable it was. In the food hierarchy, anything that thrived, fluttered, and flew close to heaven was considered superior to, for instance, the knobbly beets that grew under the ground. The so-called food of lords was also improved with all manner of expensive spices, which had first been brought back by crusaders returning from the Middle East and had since reached the country via long-distance trade. The dishes of the elite were fragrant with saffron, ginger, sugar, cinnamon, cloves, and almonds. Meanwhile, the quality of the food that found its way onto peasants' tables was much poorer. Even so, people of all ranks would still eat together on the farm—the shame of the privileged appears to be the preserve of modern human beings with their tendency toward the sentimental.

It's now dinnertime on a big estate. The tables are arranged in concentric circles. The lord of the manor sits in the middle, surrounded by his most intimate followers. Around him sits everyone who works for him—the farther away you sit, the less significant you are within the manor's social structure. The group is in high spirits; crude jokes are rewarded with uproarious laughter. (Binge eating in times of plenty, spoiled food, and renewed food shortages persistently lead to gastrointestinal suffering, which is why the shared humor often makes use of the less subtle set of topics surrounding eating and digestion.) The peasants seated at the tables farther away from the lord of the manor eat dark, hard bread made from rye, barley, or oat flour, which would not even have been sieved, leaving it full of bran and hard to chew. This peasant bread could also be found on the tables of the more privileged diners, who would use the bone-dry loaves as plates for their meat. On some occasions, once they had finished eating, they would magnanimously hand these loaves—now thoroughly soaked in the roasting juices of good meat—back to the tables farther out.

On this day, the lucky few at the table in the middle will be served a particularly popular "lord's dish": *Blamensir*, a dish composed entirely of white ingredients (and also known by the French name blancmanger). Like all the recipes described in *The Book of Good Food*, the instructions for making blamensir are somewhat fuzzy when it comes to quantities, ingredient preparations, and cooking times—instead, the author likes to end a recipe with a laconic invitation to not oversalt the dish. The book is aimed at experienced cooks who require little more than a reminder of a given recipe, and who may not be keen to share their knowledge, even if the introduction to the book claims that it will make "the unknowing cook wise." Ultimately, each recipe gives the impression that the author is standing next to the hearth in a castle kitchen while a panicked cook barks staccato instructions as he grinds spices with a mortar and pestle.

Blamensir is prepared something like this: Take half a pound of almonds and a quarter pound of rice—so far, so precise. Grind the rice into meal and pound the almonds in a mortar. Once these ingredients are finely powdered, add cold goat's milk. Next, pluck and chop a chicken breast and add it to the mixture, then add lard. Cook the mixture with plenty of heat. It's fair to assume that the mixture must be boiled. Then a kitchen boy will tug on a chain that is connected to a hoist over the fire, sending the pot rattling upward. This reduces the heat so the liquid will simmer ever so slightly and thicken (other parts of the text make reference to "thick almond milk"). The pot is then removed from the heat. Crushed violet petals are added to the steaming white stew, followed by a quarter pound of sugar. By now, a sweet fragrance will be rising from the steaming pot and the blamensir will be ready.

The recipe signs off with the suggestion that pike can be used instead of chicken during Lent.

This blend of sweet and savory ingredients may sound unappetizing to modern palates, but in the Middle Ages it was far from rare. The notion of sorting dishes according to different flavors and serving them up in succession, such that the sweet dessert emerged only at the very end of the meal, did not come into fashion until the seventeenth century. Diners could quite happily enjoy a piece of confectionery alongside some peppery game, savoring the sweet with the bitter.

Lotus Blossom Carved from a Watermelon
Sukhothai Kingdom

King Rama II, ruler of Thailand in the early nineteenth century, once wrote a poem about a queen who was banished from the courts of Siam. Despairing over the difficult situation she had found herself in, she disguised herself as a maid and snuck into the palace kitchens. Once there, she set to work. She wanted to contact her son, the prince, who was sitting unsuspectingly in the dining hall. The vegetables that were due to be added to his soup sat ready nearby, carefully cut into bite-size pieces. The banished queen pulled out her delicate little knife and began to carve intricate miniatures into the vegetables: simple scenes and memories from their shared lives as mother and son. Once she had finished, she got her hands on the vibrant fruits to be served as dessert and, again, carved pictures that might remind her son of the mother he had all but forgotten. In this story, food serves as a medium of communication—and there's a happy ending, too. As soon as the young prince recognizes the elaborate carvings, he rushes into the kitchens where he finds the outcast queen and ensures her return to the court.

The art of fruit carving, or *kae sa luk*, emerged in the courts of the Sukhothai Kingdom in Thailand, one of the world's most important centers of Buddhism, in the fourteenth century. Rambling temple complexes extended in every direction of the gently rolling landscape, and slender brick towers shaped like elongated bells cast reflections in still waters dotted with floating pink lotus blossoms. The young kingdom's ceramicists made vessels covered with shimmering jade-green glazes, which were roundly admired. Likewise, fruit carving techniques are deeply rooted in Thailand's national identity and were supposedly invented by a lady of the court by the name of Nang Nophamas, who was a skilled craftswoman.

This is another area where historiography merges with dreamlike myth—two myths, in this case. The first takes place under the rule of King Rama Khamhaeng prior to his death in 1317. On a boat trip, the king observed a lady of the court making a lantern from banana leaves, shaping the leaves so cleverly that they took on the shape of a lotus blossom. She placed a lit candle in the center of the blossom and floated it on the water under the full moon. The king was so moved by the sight of this that he took this lady—Nang Nophamas—for his wife and declared the night of the full moon in the twelfth lunar month to be a Buddhist holiday. Loy Krathong, the festival of lights, is celebrated in Thailand to this day and sees tiny rafts made from the trunk of the banana tree decorated with candles, incense sticks, flowers, and leaves released into the water. The little lanterns are thought to drive away anger and resentment.

The second legend regarding the invention of kae sa luk takes place half a century later. In this story, Nang Nophamas was a lady of the court under King Phra Ruang, a later king of the Sukhothai period. Once again, the story focuses on the celebration of Loy Krathong, but here it was already a traditional festival. Again, Nophamas made her intricate, boat-like lotus blossom from banana leaves, but this time she decorated the floating lantern with wonderful fruit and vegetable carvings. The king was so delighted by this work of art that he elevated its status to that of a court art, one all noble women were expected to learn.

It's unclear which of the two legends comes closest to historical fact. What's clear from both stories, however, is that fruit carving is, at its core, a royal art, directly bound to veneration of the Buddha—this is evidenced not just by the fact that the festival of lights is a Buddhist ceremony but the fact that, in both stories, Nang Nophamas makes a lotus blossom, the flower of the Buddha.

There is also something deeply meditative about the craft of carving. Using a small carving knife resembling a sharp quill, you cut fine grooves, uniform curves, and waves into the flesh of the fruit. And repeat. Watermelons are particularly well suited for carving oversize lotus blossoms thanks to their fresh pink color that fades to white and then green at the outer edge. Paper-thin blossoms emerge in lush pink and the edges of the leaves glow like they have been dipped in milky white paint. The swirl of blossoms grows denser toward the middle. As the next fruits are carved, the sweet scent of melon intensifies. They may be carved into fruit baskets, lined with colorful balls of other fruits. Papayas are carved to reveal blousy roses and chrysanthemums. Hard pumpkins boast carvings of twined leaves. A hand-carved garden emerges in reverse, made from the natural fruits of trees and the earth.

Creating an edible table decoration becomes a spiritual practice. Again, food is symbolically charged, standing now for religious devotion. Yet it also stands for an earthly show of power: For centuries, the ephemeral artworks created with kae sa luk have graced the King's table. (In the present day, chopping fruit and vegetables is a skill taught in cookery schools and carved fruits and vegetables now adorn the tables of ordinary people, too, as an aesthetic that is an integral component of Thai cuisine). Often, carved fruits were not even eaten and were simply admired, similar to the just-for-show dishes common in Europe during the same era. The Sukhothai Kingdom clearly harbored a desire to put more than "just" delicious food on the tables of the elite. The higher up the hierarchy, the more abundance could be found on the dining table—in the hope of making people forget that the King himself was just another human being with a digestive tract, who needed to get food into his body. Decorative dishes were superfluous, their only purposes beauty and opulence, which enabled them to conceal and outshine this fundamental truth and allowed the ruling classes to appear superhuman. And yet these flowers, carved from fruit and vegetables, seem more delicate and subtler than the gilded swans and trussed-up boars' heads that graced the tables of European princes—a fittingly humble Buddhist adornment.

Curry
India

Since time immemorial, humans have been cooking, eating, and dreaming of spices. As early as antiquity, the Phoenicians, Romans, Greeks, and Chinese were braving storms and impassable deserts on ships and sulky camels to buy pepper, ginger, and cinnamon on the Indian Malabar Coast. These spices were traded as precious commodities back home. Kingdoms went to war to gain the upper hand in the spice trade. Determined explorers set off to discover new and faster sea routes and experience incredible things. Christopher Columbus "discovered" America by accident in just this way. Vasco da Gama mastered the ocean route around the Cape of Good Hope, proving that the Atlantic was connected to the Indian Ocean and unexpectedly outwitting the Arab spice guild. Ferdinand Magellan was the first to circumnavigate the world (or, at least, the rest of his fleet was—Magellan himself was killed by the inhabitants of a Filipino island during one of his attempts to convert them to Christianity). Each of these expeditions made in the name of the spice trade fundamentally changed the Western understanding of the world. The longing for the fragrances of cinnamon and cumin and the spicy tingle of pepper was so great that it saw new continents rise up out of the water and whole oceans collide.

In India, right at the epicenter of the trade, people had always used plenty of spices in their cooking. Sanskrit texts over three thousand years old record the use of pepper and cumin and detail their medicinal effects. In India, people know about the healing power of food, a concept known as Ayurveda. Curry—which at first simply meant a versatile, spiced, strongly seasoned stew-like dish using vegetables or meat and served with rice—has likely been cooked in India for at least as long. Yet this dish, with its polyphony of spices, did not experience its heyday until much later, in the era of the Muslim Mughals who ruled India between the sixteenth and nineteenth centuries.

Like an Indian version of the Medicis, the Mughals promoted art and the delights of gastronomy. The whole world gazed in awe at the Taj Mahal and its marble façades set with gemstones, twinkling and glistening in the hot shimmering air. At the same time, brigades of cooks traversed the land alongside the imperial armies to cook for Mughal commanders. Sumptuous feasts were laid on in the Mughal courts, with gorgeous, fragrant dishes served on golden trays. Dishes would be scattered with wafer-thin leaves of real silver, which were so light that they would dance in the warm air and float down onto the long table, shimmering as they went. And so, the clamor for the rulers' favorite dishes—including curries—soon spilt over into every small garrison town.

Curries were diverse dishes in thick, gleaming sauces, glowing in all the colors of the sunset. The core of the dish would always be meat, fish, or vegetables, which would be cooked in a creamy liquid. This might contain coconut, yogurt, stock, water, or cream. But what really mattered were the spices, which so many people across the world risked their lives to acquire. Indian curries included around twenty of these sought-after ingredients on average, usually including cloves, peppercorns, cinnamon, ginger, cardamom, coriander, cumin, bay leaves, and fenugreek. Every bite of the finished dish should be sweet and sour, mild, and tangy. The spices were ground, roasted, and some mixed, just before cooking, while others were added to the gently simmering curry one at a time; every cook would play to their own tune. Later in the cooking process, the cook might fry a handful of some spices in hot oil and then drizzle it over the dish to give it an added intensity.

And then came the chile. When many people think of Indian cuisine, chile is what comes to mind: a hot, burning spiciness, enough to simultaneously scorch many a Westerner's tongue, take their breath away, and bring tears to their eyes. In fact, though Indian curries were always boldly seasoned usually with ginger and peppercorns, they were fairly mild in terms of heat until Columbus "discovered" America and, with it, chile peppers. This moment marked a turning point for the flavors of Indian, Southeast Asian, and African cooking. The Portuguese took these peppers—which tasted hotter than anything they had ever known—to Africa, the Middle East, Thailand, Japan, and India, where a particularly fiery variety, *bhut jolokia*, became a firm favorite. Thus, from the sixteenth century onward, curries became spicy, with the intensity varying by region.

Chiles arrived in India at the time when another paradigm shift was gradually taking place in Europe: a move away from peppery, highly spiced foods toward milder, buttery, creamy dishes. The contrast that developed between mild and spicy national cuisines still exists to this day.

There are several theories as to why people in countries as hot as India and Thailand enjoy eating spicy foods. Anyone who's stood at a tightly packed food stall on a dusty, hot sidewalk in Bangkok with their mouth on fire can empirically refute the theory that chile somehow inures a person to the heat. There is a general assumption that hot chiles kill off dangerous bacteria in food, providing a kind of disinfectant effect. Chiles do contain a kind of antibacterial substance, but scientific studies have shown this to be more of a pleasant side effect than a reason why certain countries love hot spice. Perhaps there's no real conclusion to this question. But this much is certain: In the era when new worlds were being discovered and previously unknown sea routes were being sailed, a number of the most varied tastes, cultures, and products united for a moment, before many of them separated again. But it was at precisely this moment that spicy curry came into the world, gleaming and colorful, fiery hot, borne on a melody of spices—and peppers.

Twelve Ounces of Solid Food, Fourteen Ounces of Wine
Italy

In the first book of his *Discorsi intorno della vita sobria*, or *Discourses About the Sober Life*, which he began transcribing around 1550 CE, Alvise Cornaro declared that he had decided to write about the vice of immoderacy in eating and drinking.[8] Born in Venice in the latter half of the fifteenth century, Cornaro already had a fair amount of life experience under his belt. A distant relation of one of the richest families in the mighty and magnificent lagoon city, he had a whale of a time . . . at first. Until he was almost forty, he was a hedonistic Renaissance man who could be found frequenting every one of the city's festivities, indulging in all bodily pleasures with abandon. At some point, he became so overweight, plagued by gout and probably diabetes, that his doctors predicted he would soon be dead. The only thing that might still save him was a radical change in diet.

And so began Cornaro's second life as an advocate for moderation. Every day for the rest of his life, Cornaro ate less than twelve ounces of solid, simple food (egg, bread, or soup) and never drank more than two small glasses of red wine. In this way, he managed to lead a healthy and unusually long life for his time—some sources claim he lived to be over one hundred years old, while others make reference to a good eighty years or so. His treatise became a kind of anti-aging bestseller, translated into several languages, and was still being consulted in the nineteenth century. It was, if you will, the original diet handbook.

Since the time of Ancient Greece, humanity has been aware of the direct relationship between food and health and has known that food can even have healing properties. It was in Greece that the term "diet" emerged from a word that meant "lifestyle" and signified a balanced relationship between the body and food. The word has since been transformed: Today, if someone speaks of a diet, they usually mean eating less. And since the late nineteenth century, this has tended to be for aesthetic reasons rather than health-related ones. "The human body is a social phenomenon through and through," writes Robert Gugutzer. "What human beings do with their bodies, the attitudes they have to them and the understanding they have of them, is shaped by culture, society, and the age in which these bodily practices, perceptions and evaluations arise."[9] Until this time, the idea of a voluntarily starved body being a societal ideal of beauty was a marginal phenomenon. This may well have been because, until then, people all over the world were regularly confronted with famine. Today's notion of the diet is also a phenomenon of affluent societies—only people who know they have a well-stocked pantry at home will go hungry willingly. Until the turn of the twentieth century, men were expected to be athletic or well-built, while women were expected to be well rounded, with fashionably slim waists—though these required corsets, not starvation diets.

One of the first extreme cases of dieting to come to the public's attention was that of the poet Lord Byron. In his diaries, Lord Byron writes in meticulous detail of his ongoing painstaking attempts to lose weight. He notes that he is eating no more than two rusks (hard biscuits) per day, along with a cup of tea once daily—he drinks apple cider vinegar the rest of the day to suppress his appetite and takes laxatives and painfully hot baths. Similarly, some decades after Byron, the Austrian Empress known as Sisi avoided food and exercised excessively in her struggle to remain the "most beautiful" woman of the age. (Up until this point, beauty was not considered an explicitly feminine matter; the male body was considered aesthetically pleasing in antiquity, and beauty remained a concern for the elite, expressed in increasingly expensive fashions that both men and women would wear, until the early eighteenth century.)

Lord Byron and Empress Sisi exhibited all the symptoms of an illness that still haunts our society. "No swill for me; I'm not a cow / I will not eat it—loathe it now; / I can't! I won't! I shan't, I vow!" cries Soupy-Kaspar in

Struwwelpeter (1844), which makes unrestricted use of poisonous pedagogy. This bedtime story of a little boy who didn't want his dinner ends as you might expect, with the boy growing thinner and thinner: "The fourth day came, and here you see / How doth this little busy bee; / He weighed perhaps a half a pound— / Death came and tucked him in the ground."[10] For one thing, the text is testament to the incredible anger prompted by a child refusing to eat—incomprehensible to adults to whom the fear of famine was all too familiar. But it's also possible to read "Soupy-Kaspar" as an early case study of a newly recognized illness—its author, after all, is Heinrich Hoffmann, a doctor and psychiatrist. In 1870, pathological starvation was given a name: anorexia nervosa. The fact that a person must eat to survive is a constant terror for sufferers of anorexia, whose numbers continue to rise in the present day. Food becomes the enemy; the body becomes disputed terrain that must be monitored on all fronts daily with a merciless eye.

Standardized clothing sizes were introduced around 1900, making it possible to clearly define a diet's aims: People wanted to starve themselves to drop two dress sizes, to finally fit a size 8, go from XL to M, and so on. The measure of deliberate hunger could now be easily quantified. And so, in the twentieth century (with a brief interruption for the war years), people outdid themselves with outrageous diet concepts: soap was thought to "wash" you slim, and then there were electric shocks, vibrating belts, tapeworms, diet pills with harmful side effects, vodka mixed with arsenic or strychnine, and a constant flow of new tips about what to eat and how much.

In comparison to most of this modern advice, Cornaro's concept of a life of moderation looks positively sensible. At least his diet allows for a pint of red wine every day.

False Venison Roast
Holy Roman Empire of the German Nation

"The beaver is an animal / Like a seal [. . .] he has his tail in the water / As this is half flesh / and the other half is fish [. . .] Nature gave him this / That it might swim behind like a fish in the water."[11]

This is a perfectly reasonable and scientifically unassailable explanation from the author of *Koch vnd Kellermeisterey*, or *Cooking and Winemaking*, first published in 1559, as to why beavers must be considered a species of fish. The animals do indeed live in water and thanks to their scaly tails, they even swim like fish; so, this categorization endured throughout the entire Late Middle Ages and into the Early Modern period, during which it was accepted as a fact. And the reason? A sheer lust for meat.

The relationship the Christians of the Middle Ages had to food was not merely shaped by famine and sporadic feasting. It was also subject to numerous prohibitions and imperious rules, as religious fasting was required for almost a third of the year. In the forty days of fasting for Lent before Easter, as well as on Fridays, Saturdays, the eve of important holidays, the three days before Ascension Day, and on Wednesdays every three months, no meat was to be consumed, and eggs and milk products were similarly banned. Fish, on the other hand, was permissible, along with grains, vegetables, and fruit.

Originally, these special days were for commemorating Jesus's fast in the desert. Over the centuries, however, this practice degenerated into a succession of empty, rigid rituals, performed solely out of habit and fear of punishment, without doing justice to the true meaning. The whole thing led to new theological interpretations of astonishing creativity, drawing from the vast repertoire of human self-deception. When it came to cleverly reinterpreting and twisting Bible passages, the real masters were often members of the Catholic orders. And so, naturally, the precise definition of a fish became a philosophical question. On the fifth day of creation, for example, God created the animals of the water and the air. So, one could argue, in good conscience, that fish and birds—having emerged practically in the same breath—belong to the same species, and so there's nothing standing in the way of a nice roast chicken. In the early fifteenth century, the Council of Constance stated that everything that lived in the water could be considered a fish. Beavers, along with otters, crayfish, frogs, mussels, and seabirds (which could now be counted as fish for two reasons) could, therefore, be prepared as Lenten fare. Enticing aromas would waft their way out of monastery kitchens: beaver liver dumplings, roasted cormorant, or otter simmering in Burgundy would grace the menu alongside crab sausages and aspic. Yet rumors went around that these delicacies were not enough for some monks, and so attempts were made to broaden the concept of water-dwelling animals even further. There was talk of declaring pigs that had been driven into rivers or drowned in wells "creatures of the water." And it was said that an abbot once crossed himself as he faced a delicious smelling roast suckling pig, only to grant the piglet the baptism of fish: *Baptisto te carpem* ("I baptize you, carp").

Beyond this semantic nitpicking, there were a fair number of cooks perpetrating deliberate fraud. They would mince the meat and hide it from God's stern eye in pastry baked until golden or in dumplings in pretty shapes. And then there were the true culinary masters who would counter the limitations of their ingredients with increased virtuosity, giving rise to truly exquisite dishes. In *Cooking and Winemaking* there is a recipe for pike, cut into four pieces: the first piece is grilled, the second is boiled in "Wein und Würtz" (wine and spices), the third is stuffed, and, finally, the tail is baked. After cooking, the fish is then reassembled before serving. In retrospect, this fish four ways seems like a bizarrely prophetic precursor to contemporary award-winning cuisine, its chefs time and again taking on the idea of conjuring several different preparations from a single ingredient and plating them up together.

Yet the cooks of medieval Lenten cuisine had even more tricks up their sleeves. Not only can you conceal meat or pass it off as fish, you can also simulate it with dishes that perform feats of mimicry to, for instance, take on the appearance of hearty roast venison. According to *Cooking and Winemaking*, it works as follows: Marinate figs and grapes in a good wine before chopping them and mixing them with flour, salt, and herbs. With wet hands, shape the dough around a skewer and cook it over the fire. Carefully slice the false roast and arrange the slices in an attractive manner. Scatter with almonds, and sugar or fresh ginger if desired, and then baste the "roast" with butter. (The final step was only possible for those living in a congregation that had received a "butter letter" from Rome, sanctioning the use of butter during Lent for geographical regions where olive oil was not available in sufficient quantities.)

The false venison roast melts in the mouth, at once sweet, spicy, and savory. (Seasoning something beyond recognition is still a common practice today.) The wealthier the household, the more exotic—i.e., expensive—and plentiful the spices; this was how hosts demonstrated their wealth. Panting and wailing with delight, the guests would sample this veritable flavor bomb of figs, ginger, pepper, and cloves, praising its searing spice and wiping tears from their eyes: "Tastes just like meat, praise the Lord, Amen!"

Borscht

Polish-Lithuanian Commonwealth

Borscht should be sour, sweet, salty, and a little spicy. A bit earthy, too. Sour cream and dill provide a distinct tangy freshness. The vegetables and meat ought to be so densely packed inside the cooking pot that the spoon stands upright when plunged into the simmering melee. Borscht is a dish of great diversity. There are countless recipes, but no single definitive one.

You cook it the way your grandmother cooked it, and she cooked it the way her grandmother did. Every borscht recipe is also a family heirloom, its ingredients bubbling with the stories of each generation, the places they lived, and the fates they met. Its familiar scent opens the door to these memories. In Southwest Ukraine, the third day after a wedding is known as *do nevistky na borshch* ("visiting your daughter-in-law to eat borscht"). Life begins and ends with this stew (which can sometimes be a soup, too) as it is also often served at wakes.

Borscht is cooked in most Slavic countries, but it probably originated in Ukraine. In any case, the typical ingredients used for borscht in Ukraine—mixed and prepared in a kaleidoscope of combinations—are stock, beetroot, carrots, white cabbage, onions, potatoes, and pork (or beef, or chicken, depending on the region).

As far back as 1584 CE, the German merchant Martin Gruneweg was traveling through Kyiv—part of the Polish-Lithuanian Commonwealth at the time—when he remarked in his diary that the Ruthenians all cooked their own borscht, sustaining themselves almost exclusively on the dish. Initially, the dish's main ingredient was hogweed, a rampant weed, the stems and leaves of which were left to ferment for a week. The fermented liquid was used for cooking; it had a sharp, sour flavor and exuded a pungent scent. The dish's sour base notes go all the way back to the Middle Ages, to the time of Kyivan Rus', the eastern Slavic state preceding the Polish-Lithuanian Commonwealth, where it is speculated borscht truly originated. One source from the twelfth century also mentions fermented hogweed. Beetroot, which we associate with the dish today, did not come eastward from Italy until later to turn the once green soup red. It remains a simple dish, filled with the fruits of earth and pasture.

The sour soup had been cooked across the whole of Eastern Europe for centuries, in all its various forms. Then came the Soviet Union. Some said that one advantage of the long period of Communist dictatorship was the fact that Slavic cuisine wasn't watered down by passing Western European trends but was able to retain its culinary traditions. Others were of the view that the Soviet Union choked off any trace of individuality, like a hermetically sealed dome, and that its cuisine stayed gray and monotonous for seventy years, with Soviet conformity suppressing any wild, untamed flavors. When the Soviet Union collapsed, its now independent nations embarked on a search for identity. Borscht was a public commodity that nevertheless belonged to everyone individually in its own form. Everyone could identify with borscht. And perhaps it was this powerful aspect of identification that ensured that, amid senseless violence thirty years later, the borscht ultimately boiled over.

In 2019, the Russian Ministry of Foreign Affairs openly claimed that borscht was the national dish of Russia, a symbol of their national cuisine. In Ukraine, people were shocked and outraged. It was perceived as another act of appropriation from the neighboring country, which had never wanted to recognize Ukrainian independence. Borscht is so emotionally tied up with homeland, family, and childhood, that claiming it as Russian seemed to many like pure malice.

"Borscht is not just a dish, it's something that makes us who we are as Ukrainians, just like our language," said Ukrainian chef Ievgen Klopotenko. "Much has been taken away from Ukraine. But you're not getting our borscht."[12] Klopotenko founded an NGO, the Institute for Ukrainian Culture, devoted entirely to borscht. He arranged masterclasses, festivals, and a National Borscht Day. He even wants to have borscht emojis designed so the dish can become a communicative symbol and feed straight into our digital everyday language. The dish ultimately became a vehicle for civil resistance: It was Klopotenko, again, who set an even bigger campaign in motion when Ukraine applied to UNESCO to have its culture of borscht cooking added to the List of Intangible Cultural Heritage in Need of Urgent Safeguarding.

And then came February 2022, when Russia invaded Ukraine. War raged. That April, Maria Zakharova, spokesperson for the Russian Ministry of Foreign Affairs, made a bizarre appearance in front of the camera. She claimed that the Ukrainians had banned Russian cookbooks because they didn't want to share borscht with the Russians. "This is what we've been talking about the whole time," was her astounding summary. "Xenophobia, Nazism, and extremism in all its forms."[13] Food became propaganda. According to Zakharova's grotesque logic, Russia had embarked on an internationally condemned war of aggression against Ukraine because the stubborn Ukrainians insisted on clinging to their national dish.

Wars often come with symbolism. In July 2022, UNESCO went ahead with its own act of symbolism. It declared Ukrainian borscht to be an intangible artifact of cultural heritage and, more besides, it expedited the addition of the Ukrainian culture of borscht cooking to the List of Intangible Cultural Heritage in Need of Urgent Safeguarding. According to the UNESCO announcement, since the beginning of the war, the bearers of the culture had been under threat of being expelled from their communities and cultural contexts. "Destruction to the surrounding environment and traditional agriculture," it added, "has prevented communities from accessing local products, such as vegetables, needed to prepare the dish."[14] "If we protect our food, we also protect our identity," says Chef Klopotenko. "Borscht is our identity."[15] Borscht can't determine the outcome of the war, but the battle for borscht itself has been won.

Roast Swan
Europe

We see before us the Baroque garden of a European princely house. The flower beds are arranged geometrically, with gleaming red borders. A carriage, pulled by four white horses, floats between several water fountains, the jets of water shooting high up into the air. The whole scene is frozen, ossified in time. The beds, the horses, the fountains, the flowers glitter surreally in the candlelight: Everything in this scene is made out of sugar.

And now the next feasting table is presented to the guests, the showpieces laid out ceremoniously: birds complete with feathers, heads, and wings. They, too, are frozen, but not in sugar. First, a guineafowl, its spotted plumage enhanced with gold leaf. It sits in a basket made of dough, next to a peacock with its beak and eye sockets covered in gold. And then—cue excitable cheers from the guests—a snow-white swan. Its wings are raised, its beak gleaming gold. Several golden chains circle its long, curved neck.

The swan's skin and feather-coat would be removed before the flesh was roasted. Once it was cooked, the body would be reassembled and covered with its entire outer layer. A wire support, such as the one illustrated in the 1719 *Neues Salzburgisches Kochbuch*, or *New Salzburg Cookery Book*, would keep the neck and wings in position. And as we have already seen in antiquity, there might also be a couple of pie crusts, out of which birds would flutter, dogs would jump, or which might even—depending on the host's sense of humor—spring open to reveal a little person.

There was a penchant for serving these kinds of "table showpieces" at European courts in the Baroque period, an era of theatrical opulence. They were a relic from the Middle Ages and were usually served in between courses—much like contemporary theater, which relies on quick, efficient scene changes. The dining table would become a stage, the dishes served up as food for the eyes: "Such dishes are named show dinners / Made by human hand / Delightful to watch and edible as well: they first delight the eyes / And then the mouth / And are mostly laid out / When one has had sufficiency of the other dishes," explains the poet Georg Philipp Harsdörffer in his *Vollständiges und von neuem vermehrtes Trincir-Buch*, or *The Complete and Newly Expanded Book on Carving* (1657).[16]

The reason why the roast swan wasn't eaten when the guests sat down at the table, hungry and full of anticipation for the culinary delights to come, became clear the moment the noble bird was freed from its mantle and sliced. The meat was tough and tasted blandly of nothing. Even valiant attempts at seasoning could do little to counter the queasy feeling of chewing on a piece of tired old flesh. And the sugar gardens and structures due to be enjoyed for dessert would not have been any more palatable; they were simply sweet and only good, perhaps, if you were aware of the painstaking effort that had gone into the artwork dissolving on your tongue. Harsdörffer also writes of "images made of butter" but is quick to concede that they started to smell or even go rancid rather swiftly, and that there was also, of course, the risk of them melting.

In the seventeenth century, table manners became more refined, a development that was accompanied by a proliferation of instruments required for these grand table settings; tablecloths and an ever-changing selection of cutlery covered the table. Napkins were elaborately folded into birds, fish, and buildings, and the tablecloth might also be draped in a series of waves and swirls to create a mountain landscape or a textile ocean. These tablescapes were littered with yet more luxurious objects: fine, shimmering glasses, gleaming golden cups, plates and dishes, and heavy platters would rise amidst table fountains filled with perfumed water.

Show dishes are yet another ostentatious addition to the theater of table settings, intended—as the name suggests—to provoke astonishment in the viewers. Much like the optical illusion of Baroque still-life paintings, in which the virtuosity with which the objects are depicted baffles the viewer, in this case, it was less a matter of taste than of the purely overwhelming visual experience that greeted the eye—the golden beaks, gleaming feathers, dramatically outstretched wings, and daintily decorated swan necks. This probably also explains why diners at these banquets tolerated the fact that the "normal" dishes, prepared to a similar degree of refinement, also tasted rather mediocre. Due to the increased fire risk, the kitchens would be located far from the dining hall, and finished dishes would have to be hauled through a number of oversize suites of rooms. And even though many castles had several ovens for reheating dishes along the obstacle course between the kitchen and dining hall, the food would generally be lukewarm at best by the time it arrived at the table and would often be served cold. Once again, presentation—just like the impressive effect of many huge rooms—was more important than the taste of a well-cooked meal.

The year 1761 saw an abrupt end to the habit of creating show dishes from edible ingredients when Empress Maria Theresa banned the use of food for wasteful purposes. Yet the swans, boars' heads, and peacocks continued to appear at table; they were simply transformed into fine-worked faience earthenware. They were accompanied by astonishingly real-looking turkeys, daintily elaborate fish, or heads of Savoy and red cabbage, their colors and delicate surface details reproduced in fragile porcelain. These sculptural false dishes

would turn out to be hollow tureens, concealing delicious dumplings or sweet surprises. The eyes no longer
needed to dine solo: Flavor was back.

Sauce
France

Butter changed everything; 1651 CE saw the publication of a revolutionary cookbook: *Le Cuisinier François*, or *The French Cook*, by François Pierre de la Varenne, who to this day is considered to be one of France's most significant cooks. The book secured a radical shift in taste, which was advancing throughout Europe at the time. This shift can be summed up in a single word: sauce. Buttery, fatty, thickened sauce.

Sauces did not play a particularly key role in the region's cuisines prior to this time, and when they were used, they were generally salty or sour. They also tended to be thin and watery. Cooks in antiquity would sprinkle extremely salty fish sauce into practically every dish, though these would almost certainly be completely over-seasoned already, having been readily scattered with pungent, bitter herbs. In the Middle Ages, sauces were occasionally thickened with bread crumbs, nuts, liver, or blood. They would otherwise comprise sour, thin ingredients like wine, vinegar, and the juice of citrus fruits or unripe grapes, and the whole thing would be heavily spiced. Such sauces were not familiar with fat. Prior to the culinary paradigm shift in the seventeenth century, cooking with spices was the epitome of good cooking, in part because spices were a precious commodity. Great explorers like Ferdinand Magellan were still losing their lives to acquire spices more quickly and in greater quantities when wealthy Europeans abruptly lost interest in ginger, cinnamon, nutmeg, and all the other intense flavors and scents of spices, because they were no longer exclusive to the upper classes.

The invention of modern sauce, however, was a triumph of butter more than anything else. Butter was increasingly available from the fourteenth and fifteenth centuries onward, as cattle farming gained in popularity. From the moment it melted on people's tongues, the taste of butter spread throughout Europe like sizzling, hot, greasy lava. The farming of milk-producing livestock boomed: Everyone wanted more butter. The French historian J. L. Flandrin wrote, "I cannot see which demographic, economic, or technological changes could explain this culinary revolution. It does not manifest on the level of material compulsion but on that of desire."[17] That was it: Butter simply tasted good. The desire and pleasure inherent to food now came to the fore.

La Varenne and other cooks of his ilk developed completely new sauces out of butter, which are still found in good home cooking today. Roux was the magic ingredient that La Varenne employed to create thick, silky-textured sauces. This previously unknown method of combining fat with starch lent runny, thin sauces viscosity and body. Take béchamel sauce, for example: Put butter in a hot pan, let it melt and heat up, then add flour while stirring, and the two will bind together to create a creamy, pale paste. Now add milk, stirring all the time, and an off-white sauce will emerge, heavy and dense, with only a very delicate scent and flavor. It doesn't add flavor to the dish, but instead takes on the flavors of the accompanying ingredients.

This was another part of the shift in tastes: Food was no longer a bitter, sour, heavily seasoned explosion of flavor. Delicate, mild, and fresh flavors were now flooding the dinnerplates of Europe. Truffles, mushrooms, chives, and shallots were combined with creamy sauces. What's more, La Varenne drew up the first recipes for vegetables, which were previously not thought of as especially interesting. The true flavors of meat and fish were to be brought to the fore and properly tasted—this was a crucial tenet of new French cuisine. "Sauces are the splendor and glory of French cooking," writes Julia Child centuries later. "A sauce should never be considered as a disguise or a mask."[18] Wolfram Siebeck warns, "The point of a sauce is not to drown the potatoes, but to subtly enhance the meat!"[19] Sauce is the difficult to define, fluid element of a dish that cascades straight into the flavor center, the buttery liquid that plays around all the other components. It coats and flows, hot and gleaming, into the spaces in between, covers a roast, saturates the vegetables. It's the first thing children will spoon off their plates, the last thing to be soaked up with a hunk of bread. When people say, "I could take a bath in that," it evokes a deep dish, filled with soft, warm sauce, ready to dive into. It's the most gratuitous element of a dish, and the one we want most of all.

La Varenne's sauce cuisine would later be formalized to include the five "mother sauces": béchamel, velouté, espagnole, *tomate*, and hollandaise. The first three have a roux base. The tomato sauce is a fruity essence, made of tomato flesh and concentrated tomato paste. Hollandaise involves beating together egg yolk and butter. If you know these five sauces, you can create countless other variations of these silky basics. Out of these emerged an ever-greater number of sophisticated recipes, based on a strict school of thought; classic French cookery was born, and it would go on to become one of the world's great cuisines. And so, La Varenne did not just invent sauces—for much of the world, he redefined what good food is.

Afternoon Tea
Kingdom of England

We find ourselves in an impressive stately home, perhaps somewhere in Southamptonshire. Drizzling rain cloaks the long drive in mist, and the ample lawns and neatly clipped borders glisten wetly. Inside the manor house are suites of rooms with high ceilings. Sumptuous rugs muffle the sound of footsteps. Crystalline carafes rattle softly in the cabinets. The silver is to be touched only with gloved hands. Forebears gaze out from picture frames with an air of dignified humorlessness.

Inside one of these rooms sits the lady of the house, attending to her present task with utter concentration. She is preparing tea for her guests. The job is too important, and the tea too expensive, to leave to the staff. Consequently, she has the only key to the tea caddy, a small chest made of polished wood, decorated with inlays like a jewelry box. This is where the much-prized tea leaves are stored.

The other paraphernalia stand waiting on a silver tray: a kettle with hot water just off the boil, a teapot heated with a little hot water, a tea strainer, a jug of milk, a pot of sugar, and lemon slices on a small glass plate. The lady of the house opens the box, scoops out some tea with a silver spoon, and tips it into the teapot. One teaspoon per person, and one for the pot. She then pours over the hot water, her face tense with concentration. An air of ritual solemnity grips the whole room. There's a crackle as the first drops of water hit the dry leaves, and fragrant steam rises out of the pot. Now for the cups. These are made of china, delicately painted with flowers and birds. They are so paper-thin that the milk must be added to each cup first; if boiling water is poured straight into one of these fragile vessels, the cup will shatter on the spot.

Writer and dramatist Eduard von Keyserling once wrote, "If England were granted global domination, it would also mean the global dominance of afternoon tea and the English lounge chair."[20] In fact, afternoon tea quickly developed into a sense of national identity; it was quintessentially British, and not just from the perspective of other nations—the Brits themselves celebrated their way of life by means of this ritual. And it cut through all social classes. As early as 1750 or so, the East India Company was importing tea on a large scale, and by the mid-nineteenth century the price of tea dropped so low that even the working class was able to afford it.

Tea and its development from an elitist drink to an egalitarian afternoon meal—for these days a proper afternoon tea includes solid food—were closely tied to the role of women in English society. When the Portuguese princess Catarina de Bragança came to England in 1662 to marry Charles II she brought with her a small caddy of tea, inadvertently associating tea with royalty and setting off a trend. Coffee, which had previously been the hot beverage of choice, was soon replaced by tea; by around 1700, tea was already the preferred drink of the upper classes.

Though the lady of the house bore sole responsibility for storing and preparing the tea in her own house, she was not permitted to linger in public coffeehouses, which also served tea. When the first teashops opened in the early eighteenth century, ladies would wait at the back door while their male servants placed their orders inside the shop. Not long afterward, however, the first tea gardens emerged, small parks free of the stricter rules governing enclosed spaces, and it was here where women could finally meet outside the home to drink tea. It was a huge step away from socially prescribed domestic isolation. The tea gardens disappeared again toward the end of the century (one might imagine this had something to do with the English weather), but tea and female socializing had by then become inextricably linked. It was common for women to meet for afternoon tea in their living rooms—indeed, you can read about it in detail in any Jane Austen novel. And so, this hot drink rendered the most private of spaces semi-public, places where crucial social interactions would play out.

Afternoon tea would go on to experience yet another uptick in appreciation. In the Victorian era, from around 1840 onward, small bites began to be served alongside tea, an innovation allegedly introduced by another woman, the Duchess of Bedford, a lady-in-waiting to the Queen. Small sandwiches, sponge cakes, jam-filled Bakewell tart, and—of course—scones became part of this carefully fostered ritual of the British Empire, until five o'clock tea ultimately represented a meal in its own right, with its own customs and rules of etiquette. It gave rise to the tea dress, a garment with a comfortable fit, which was worn without a corset; it was the first time that English women appeared in company without being laced into corsetry.

Food has been swathed in ritual throughout human history. This works particularly well because human beings have to eat in order to survive; food is so closely tied up with our existence that the leap to ritual—a constantly repeated process—is a small one. Afternoon tea, with its perfect little cakes and the aromatic subtleties of the expensive hot drink at its heart, rises above the mundanity of merely ingesting food. Afternoon tea is, in its origins, a luxurious ritual—a meal with the power to define identity, for a nation no less, and one that emerged with imperialist aplomb.

Elsewhere, Keyserling writes that, for the English, comfort is a national asset. He describes the relentless perfectionism with which the Brits arrange their surroundings and organize their habits; he calls this a "machinery for a life of harmony," and one that takes up an unnaturally large space in the everyday lives of the English.[21] To this day, the global domination of afternoon tea, silver milk jugs, tea caddies, and lounge chairs is celebrated in private the world over.

Potatoes Cooked in Their Skins
Kingdom of Prussia

Rain. Constant rain. The rain pours from the heavens with grueling monotony. First, there's a long, wet summer, where the fields grow sodden and the grain lies senseless in the mud. Then comes winter, harsh and icy cold. The land is white until well into spring. Then the much-feared summer rains return once more. The corn drowns in sludge. Thereafter follows another long winter, and another summer deluged by rain. The sky remains dull and gray. It's a climate catastrophe, lasting almost three years, brought about by various climatic anomalies. Persistent rain in Europe. Spoiled harvests from France to Ukraine, Scandinavia to Switzerland. The same climatic anomalies cause extreme drought in Central America, India, and large swaths of Africa. Millions of people go hungry and starve. Epidemics break out. Misery and violence rule the streets.

At the same time that this apocalyptic scenario unexpectedly settled over humanity, the potato was on the ascent in Europe. But let's start at the beginning.

From the 1520s onward, the Spanish conquistadors began their conquest of the Incan Empire in South America. On their first raids, cheerfully named "exploration trips," they happened upon enormous, concentric terraces that extended partway into the mountains. In the soil, they found tubers of bizarre beauty, in countless shapes and colors: rutted, dark purple balls; slim, golden yellow crescents; dark brown oblongs reminiscent of sausages; knobbly cones dotted with red. Some were striped, others spotted. Before sowing these strange plants—potatoes— the Incas would hold elaborate ceremonies in their fields. They even fashioned clay vessels in the same plump shape as the tubers. After the harvest, the potatoes would be laid out in the uplands, where they would freeze like hard stones. The Incas would then crush the moisture out of the frozen clumps with their feet and leave them to dry in the sun. Treated this way, the tubers would keep for up to fifteen years. They were a nourishing food and particularly suitable as traveling fare. Wide-eyed, the conquistadors grabbed some of the unfamiliar plants to take home. Potatoes were coming to Europe.

Once the potatoes arrived, they initially found themselves on the plates of the upper classes, as a kind of exotic curiosity. Years of research and cultivation would follow. At some point, varieties that were easy to grow and resistant to cool, rainy weather were cultivated. However, these first varieties didn't taste particularly good, even to the far-from-pampered palates of the simple folk, who still mainly lived off hard bread and porridge, both made from rye and oats. These first European potatoes tasted sour and watery.

And that's where the problems began. People didn't like these potatoes. Yet forward-thinking scientists and heads of state spotted the tubers' potential. Potatoes could produce very high yields and grow without issue even in difficult climate conditions. They were healthy, filling, and cheap. They had the potential to rid the world of one of the greatest threats of the modern era: hunger.

The people of Prussia greeted the potatoes with utmost suspicion. However, their king, Friedrich II, had realized long ago—after his great-grandfather had the plant cultivated in the Berlin Lustgarten—the important role these "potatoes" could play. He was determined, despite all resistance, to popularize them among the public. Friedrich the Great's "Potato Orders" are one of the first examples of the procurement of food becoming a social and political matter. In this way, Friedrich was very much a ruler of the Enlightenment, according to which public good was understood as a duty of the state.

Nevertheless, the enlightened populace immediately became a nuisance because Friedrich's plan didn't go smoothly. In his autobiography, Joachim Nettelbeck writes of the rocky path the Potato Order had to walk in the 1740s.

A large freight wagon full of potatoes arrived at the marketplace. In the town and suburbs, drums were beaten to announce that every person who owned a garden should find their way to the town hall at a specific time, because His Majesty the King intended to grant them a special blessing. [. . .] There were now more men standing outside the town hall than the whole number of these new fruits put together. Elaborate instructions were read out detailing how the potatoes were to be planted and cultivated. [. . .] However, the good people took the prized tubers in their hands, smelt them, tasted them, and licked them. [. . .] They broke them apart and threw them to the dogs nearby, who sniffed at them before losing interest. Now they had received their verdict.[22]

And so, the potato's progress stalled at first. Friedrich complained angrily about his unruly subjects: "Since We heard that the obstinacy of the servant folk, refusing as they do to eat the *potatoes* for the reason that their forefathers did not each of such, is severely setting back the cultivation of those same fruits."[23]

It was this situation that gave rise to the Potato Orders, public orders and circular letters with titles such as *Circular Opposing the Refusal of the Servant Folk to Eat Potatoes.*[24]

Filled with frustration, Friedrich the Great might have said, "A farmer will not eat what he doesn't know." In Germany today, this is a common adage, and it refers to a fundamental phenomenon: For many, food is the embodiment of familiarity. Unknown dishes are often met with mistrust, and this may be evolutionary; after all, an unfamiliar tuber could be poisonous. Foreign food is often truly accepted only once a larger group of people has culturally appropriated it in some form.

And so it was with the unfamiliar tuber from the distant empire of the Incas. The trigger was the dramatic famine that took place from 1770 to 1772. The people who had gone ahead and planted a few potatoes were the only ones with crops to harvest. This made an impression, and the German potato campaign began gaining momentum. Having the potato crop to rely on warded off hunger in many places—and freed the common people from the sludgy monotony of grain porridge for the first time in millennia.

Shortly after the starvation crisis ended, the King was pleased to receive reports that the people were now happily eating potatoes. A particular favorite dish was warm potatoes cooked in their skins, with a side of bread and butter; the earthy, slightly sweet taste of the potatoes went perfectly with the smooth mildness of the fatty butter. However, a well-meaning encyclopedia from 1785 recommended that servants serve potatoes only in the evenings to avoid spending too much time peeling them for breakfast or lunch.

There's always *something*.

Picnic

France and the United Kingdom

It's a bright spring day in the year 1789, perhaps. Bees buzz over the fragrant wildflower meadows, a small watermill burbles quietly, and a gate squeaks as a young woman steps through. She is dressed in simple peasant garb, which hangs gracefully about her figure. The woman is Marie Antoinette, Queen of France. The Queen has had a rustic escape built in the heart of Versailles, a picturesque hamlet complete with small peasants' houses, rustic gardens, and a working dairy. It is here where she will meet with her closest friends, all dressed as shepherds and peasants, and enjoy days spent living a supposedly simpler life, close to nature—they have all read Rousseau's critiques of civilization, which argue that modern man is too estranged from nature. Meanwhile—and this would later have most unfavorable consequences for Marie Antoinette and her ilk—the real peasants beyond her palace gardens are starving and preparing to revolt. Whispers in Paris and angry voices behind closed doors in the countryside claim the young Queen's dreamworld hosts genteel outdoor feasts, with food and drink of unimaginable exclusivity brought out from the palace kitchens.

After the French Revolution, many of the aristocrats who succeeded in escaping France fled to England. They brought with them their love of *pique-nique*, which at the time, referred generally to a casual way of eating in which everyone brought something to share and could take place indoors or outdoors. In 1801, the Pic Nic Society was founded in London. The Society was made up of a troupe of thoroughly extravagant, young Francophile Brits who got together in rooms on Tottenham Street to eat, drink, be merry—and always put on a play. Each member would bring a dish with them (precisely which dish would be determined by drawing lots), plus six bottles of wine. Later, in Victorian England, picnicking al fresco—eating outdoors seated on a blanket, with a basket of goodies placed in the middle—became fashionable, delighting both the English aristocracy and the "simpler" people of the working class. The latter would be particularly happy to escape the smoggy gloom of London and its great maw of factories on their day off and settle themselves somewhere in the countryside with a simple meal. They might also be equipped with a vasculum, a flattened case perfect for another eccentric Victorian pastime: collecting a few fronds of decorative ferns and other plant specimens.

The picnic marked a sensitive point in human history: It was the first age in which people were significantly estranged from nature, while being thoroughly conscious of that fact. People were exhausted, tired of industrialization, the flood of factory-made goods, and the sight of the soot-blackened city sky. And so, they sank back onto their picnic blankets—on the ground, right on top of the sun-warmed earth with its grass stalks and ants—to enjoy an unpretentious meal free of the usual conventions.

Yet during the nineteenth century, it was precisely this innocent picnicking that increasingly became the subject of large mises-en-scène. Painters, particularly the French Impressionists, discovered a popular motif in meals enjoyed under the open sky. Such scenes had everything you could ask for: ladies in bright dresses with sunhats shifting in the breeze, a small gathering in the sun-dappled light of a green forest, and attractive foods such as French pastries and colorful fruits, offering up a still life on a pretty blanket. Édouard Manet's *Le Déjeuner sur l'herbe* ("The Luncheon on the Grass") prompted an outright scandal, depicting a picnic attended by two fully clothed men accompanied by a completely naked woman sitting on the forest floor. A small basket filled with cherries and a few brioches has fallen to one side and some of the contents have rolled out, but nobody has attempted to tidy up the mess. (This certainly would not have happened if they had been using the Victorian invention of the English picnic basket. The basket was a popular tool for settling oneself in nature without having to do away with fine etiquette. It contained silver cutlery, crystal glasses and china plates, salt and pepper shakers, and a pretty sugar bowl, with everything scrupulously arranged and attached to the inside of the basket's lid.)

In her highly influential 1861 cookbook *Mrs. Beeton's Book of Household Management*, Mrs. Beeton lists the elements required for a successful picnic. Broadly speaking, it's a lot of meat: roast beef, ribs, roast chicken, ham, tongue, several different pies, and a boiled calf's head. And why not throw in a couple of lobsters, too? In addition to this, Beeton suggests salads, then gently preserved fruits, which transported well in sealed glass bottles, as well as fresh fruit, biscuits, cake, and puddings, and not to forget bread and butter for the tea, which could be prepared on a portable stove. Civilization had caught up with human beings once again. Even attendees at the annual horseracing at Ascot could enjoy stylish picnics.

In France, too, the *pique-nique* had evolved into an activity popular with all social classes in the belle époque. On Sundays, the people headed for the forests and parks of the Bois de Boulogne, which saw a rush of activity. A parade of dapper riders and carriages trotted along the park's paths and boulevards, and the rich were not short of fancy ideas, sometimes having their carriages pulled by ostriches or camels. In their midst, people picnicked in the meadows, with bread, cheese, and wine, regarding the spectacle of it all. It was both authentic nature and manufactured mise-en-scène: the polarity of modern man.

Canned Meat

French Empire

They have come from all over the world. The swell of people filters through the halls like a sluggish stream. Far above their heads, the glass roof seems to blaze with sunlight. Built of iron and glass, the palatial structure spans everything in sight: people, trees, crystalline water fountains, sculptures. There are huge, groaning machines, cattle and horses, a completely new kind of gadgetry known as the telegraph. At another stand, a tin can is opened amid a breathless hush. The year is 1851 and history is being made in London: The Great Exhibition is being held in the newly built Crystal Palace. Alongside all the other innovations on display here, visitors witness the ultimate proof that the tin can is the saving grace that could solve the world's hunger problem.

But let's go back in time a couple of years. At the beginning of the nineteenth century, the French confectioner Nicolas Appert discovered a way to store fruit, vegetables, and meat for longer than ever before. The food was placed in thick glass bottles, much like Champagne bottles, which were filled to the brim. Appert would then hermetically seal the bottles with a cork and heat them in a water bath. The freshness of the foodstuffs would be preserved. These bottles of preserved food were tested by the French navy. A few burst, but otherwise the crew was able to eat enjoyable food even on long voyages; all of the problems experienced by the Napoleonic armies appeared to have been solved.

In 1810, the French government gave Appert a choice: He could either have his invention patented, or he could publish his findings and receive a sum of prize money. The inventor opted for the latter, and the British happily went straight ahead and began preserving food using Appert's methods. However, they used containers made of tin, which, unlike glass, did not break easily. Appert himself also switched to tins and established his own factory.

It was one of his preserved tins, almost forty years old by this time, that was opened at the Great Exhibition before a sizable audience. In many ways, it was a time capsule of sorts. Appert had died ten years previously, yet inside the tin, time seemed to have stood still. Its contents were fresh as if they had just been preserved the previous day. Humanity had solved its greatest problem with food: spoilage. It was no longer dependent solely on the products that could be harvested in each season, and it became less reliant on short delivery routes. Now, you could slaughter a cow, preserve its meat, and eat it years

later. Of course, people had always put aside excess provisions in times of plenty, but tins of preserves could keep
any kind of food fresh in quantities that had once seemed
unthinkable.

The tinned foods inspired conquerors and explorers.
Now, not only could whole troops be fed on campaigns,
but ordinary people could also set out into unfamiliar
terrain, pushing on ever farther with their tinned foods
in tow. So began the ambitious polar expedition under Sir
John Franklin in 1845, planned to last three years. When
the ships left England, they had provisions for this extended period on board, including 15,600 pounds (7,100
kg) of fresh canned meat and almost 10,500 pounds (4,740
kg) of canned potatoes and vegetables.

Shortly after the celebrated opening of Appert's long-
stored can, however, the sad news arrived that all 129
participants on the voyage had died. One possible cause
was poisoning from the lead used to solder the cans shut
at that time. Even on a later polar voyage under George
W. DeLong, there were reports than the men would find
themselves biting into small balls of lead when trying to
eat cans of tomatoes, whereupon they would joke that
someone must have been hunting the tomatoes with a
shotgun. Though this was obviously not the case, the cans
were regularly hacked at with bayonets—it was the only
way to get into the thick-walled cans, as can openers had
yet to be invented. Hammers and chisels were also used.
In many households, women would melt the solder away
using an iron. However, despite these trials and their

lethal repercussions, there was no stopping the triumphal march of the tin can. By the turn of the century, they were already being produced on a large scale.

In 1962, Andy Warhol painted cans of Campbell's soup—thirty-two varieties to be exact, every flavor of Campbell's canned soup available at the time. He presented the paintings to a largely uncomprehending public arranged on shelves of the kind found in the supermarket: Canned food had long since become a product of consumer society. Now, ready meals were being preserved, too. The can needed only to be quickly opened (by now, can openers had been invented) and its contents swiftly heated. After millennia of devoting almost the entire day to procuring and preparing food, modern humans could now spend only a fraction of their time on it. This time saving, however, came at the cost of variety in taste. Even though there were thirty-two varieties of canned soup, cans of food were prepared and filled on an industrial scale, and every can tasted the same as the next. The result was a standardization of food. A consistently sized portion would be sealed inside a metal capsule that would keep light and air from reaching the contents until they were ultimately released with a gentle hiss. On opening, an intense aroma would emanate from the can, concentrated, almost unpleasant. Cold food does not smell as tempting as a soup on a slow boil. It does not release aromas like a simmering stew; instead, it breathes a frozen version of its flavors into the air. A tinned meal resembles homemade food only once it has been heated.

Warhol claimed that he had had the same lunch—canned soup—every day for twenty years, according to his estimates. This was conformity not just as an artistic principle but also as the anti-taste experience of the industrial age.

In the present day, upscale cuisine is discovering the art of preserving for itself. These are not industrially preserved foods, but foods preserved and cured on an intimate scale; intensely flavored and scented products cloaked in a subtle broth. This makes it possible to create deliciously unlikely dishes, including combinations of fruits and vegetables from different seasons, like a savory winter cabbage paired with the summer freshness of strawberries. And homemade preserves suddenly have something romantic about them, a touch of community gardens and the dream of self-sufficiency—and hope in hard times.

After enabling humankind to explore the world at the beginning of their triumphal march across our plates, canned foods now facilitate a total withdrawal from the world. Germany's Federal Office for Civil Protection and Disaster Assistance recommends maintaining a constant emergency stockpile of food provisions to last ten days. Sometimes, escapism comes in a can.

Nigiri Sushi

Japan

A brief nod, a deep breath, and then the two fishermen hoist up the enormous tuna. They use several ropes to tie it to a pole. The great fish swings and smacks against their bodies as they hurry along, the bottoms of their striped, light cotton kimonos gathered up to keep them from stumbling in the crowd. Above their heads hang large baskets filled with seabream and abalone, reminiscent of rustic stone ears. Octopus tentacles hang down limply, like tired cords on a beaded curtain. Suddenly, the cries of the busy fishermen and traders are drowned out by the ringing of countless shrill little bells—the day begins at six in the morning. Outside the fish market, the streets of the city are waking up, too. At this time, the city is one of the largest in the world. This is Edo, known in the present day as Tokyo.

When the Tokugawa Shogunate took power in Japan in 1603, it marked the imminent end of a long period of unrest for the island nation. This was due to an unusual decision: As the whole world was changing, with new countries being explored and great trade routes emerging, Japan chose to seal itself off entirely from the rest of the planet. For over two hundred years, almost no foreigners were allowed to enter the country, and Japan's residents were not allowed to leave. Its sole contact with a few select trading partners took place on an artificially raised island off the port of Nagasaki; other than this, the country remained under a bell jar.

But how would a country that had broken away so resolutely from all external influences develop? As it happened, Japan's self-created bubble released unexpected energies—to this day, the Edo period is considered a golden age of Japanese culture, particularly where culinary matters are concerned. While peasants in Central Europe were still supping glumly on their grain porridge, Edo's rice farmers were enjoying silky soups with buckwheat noodles, grilled eel with sweet kabayaki sauce, and fragrant tempura (as a Buddhist nation, meat-eating was forbidden). This period of total isolation also saw the emergence of a dish so unique that its like had never been seen or tasted elsewhere in the world: sushi.

It began with a special fermentation method. As early as the sixth century, people in Japan were packing fish and salt into barrels along with cooked rice. Centuries later, this process evolved to include seasoning the rice with rice vinegar and pressing it into wooden molds together with the fish. Even in the Edo period, this early sushi was already popular. It was predominantly sold in street stalls, small wooden booths like miniature houses. The stalls were everywhere; on the side of the road and at crossings, outside much-frequented bathhouses—there were thousands of them. At night, their colorful paper lanterns would glimmer over the heads of the passing crowds. Visitors to the stands would eat standing up, dunking the bite-size pieces into a large communal dish of soy sauce. Afterward, they would wipe their hands on a soft cotton cloth hanging on the stand. The more popular the stand, the dirtier the cloth.

And then, toward the end of the Edo period, sushi's form changed again. Two hundred years after the beginning of Japan's isolation, around 1830, a sushi master by the name of Yohei invented nigiri sushi. This elegant dish was the epitome of the Edo bubble's cultural developments. Rice was mixed with vinegar and sugar and shaped by hand to create small oval pieces, an organic impression of the inside of a closed hand (nigiri, which means "squeezed," takes its name from this part of the process). The upper side of the little ball would be spread with a thin layer of wasabi paste. This would be followed by a smooth, precise slice of fish or seafood, initially marinated or cooked, later fresh and raw. The influence of vegetarian cuisine had entrenched in Japanese culture a certain aversion to fatty, earthy, meaty flavors; Edo cuisine demanded clarity. It was important for diners to be able to taste every ingredient used in a dish, which was another reason why nigiri sushi was barely seasoned.

These bites of sushi emerged as precious objects of minimalist beauty, spreading throughout the Edo Shogunate, and later the rest of Japan.

The boom in the art of printing contributed significantly to the swift and accurate transfer of culinary techniques within Japan. Readers will be familiar with the colored woodblock prints created thanks to innovations in printing technology during the Edo period: warriors and ladies in colorful kimonos that flow like water; Mount Fuji surrounded by a froth of cherry blossoms; snow-covered Japanese villages; glimpses into teahouses, their sliding doors opening onto wonderful gardens. Not to forget Katsushika Hokusai's iconic print *The Great Wave off Kanagawa* (created around the same time that nigiri sushi emerged), the tips of the wave flying up and away from the raging water like birds. It was the very same Hokusai who illustrated the cookbook *Edo ryūkō ryōri tsū taizen*, or *The Handbook of Fashionable Cuisine for the Epicures of Edo*. Fish glide over the book's pages, wild mushrooms seem to pop up out of the paper, and the lush leaves of a radish reach for the letters beyond the book fold. This cookbook is a synthesis of the arts.

The art of making sushi finally made its way out to the wider world when Japan finally opened up in 1853. This was accompanied by an ever-growing sushi perfectionism, which has yet to reach its peak, and compared to which the sushi that trundles past diners on a little conveyer belt in fast-food restaurants is barely recognizable as the same dish. The training required to become a sushi master reveals a kind of patriarchal rigor. In the first year, all a student may do is sit in a corner, still and unmoving like a piece of furniture, as far from the master as possible, and observe what he does. Over the many years that follow, he will move his workstation closer to his master's, inch by inch. The observation stage is followed by a couple of years in which the student sharpens the knives. The master has ten knives; the *sushiya* who assists him is equipped with three knives. At some stage, the big day arrives when the student is permitted to touch the rice for the first time; he will then wash the rice and remove any imperfect grains. The process continues at this pace ... and after about fifteen years, the student will be able to make some pretty decent sushi. "You must fall in love with your work," said Jiro Ono, the most famous sushi master of recent times. This uncompromising perfectionism is the legacy of what was probably the most productive hibernation of all time.

Fish and Chips
United Kingdom

The oil bubbles and spits, simmering away in multiple vats. The hot spray sends grease into the air of the narrow room, landing on the hair and clothing of waiting customers. The little shop is situated somewhere in Britain, in an estate of terraced houses—narrow, straight streets surrounded by parades of small redbrick houses. Behind the rudimentary counter, potatoes are being cut into long sticks before being placed in the hot oil; the bubbling beast gulps them down with a cheerful hiss. Next up is the fish—a firm, white-fleshed variety like cod or haddock. The fillets are dunked with practiced ease in a shallow dish containing a batter of milk, eggs, and flour before being placed in the oil. The scent of hot, fried fish emanates into the rainy street where customers are waiting. It's Friday evening and for decades—centuries even—generations of families living here have been standing in line every Fish Friday to purchase their traditional takeaway for a couple of shillings.

Swift hands open a sheet of yesterday's newspaper and heap the hot fried fish and chips on top without much fanfare. These are sprinkled with salt, then malt vinegar, which rains down over the chips like a sour perfume. "Today's headlines, tomorrow's fish and chip paper," so goes the saying in the UK. And yes, headlines do blur; the grease makes the newspaper print run and come away from the paper and leave black marks here and there on the golden batter. In the 1990s, wrapping food in newspaper was outlawed on health grounds, but there are still nostalgic voices who claim fish and chips tasted better wrapped in newsprint. The law was primarily aimed at the takeaway dish, flecked with black ink, which would be served up every Friday out of the crackling pages of the tabloids spread across the dinner tables of Great Britain, a deeply rooted sentimental institution. Food and memory, nostalgia and identity—all of these play a significant role in this rather unassuming dish and its history.

The increasing proliferation of faster trading routes, the invention of canning and, of course, industrialization, combined in the second half of the nineteenth century to allow food to travel farther from its source than ever before, meaning people were less and less reliant on seasonal local produce. The variety of available foods grew, finally becoming accessible to the less wealthy, too. Now, dishes could be produced over again in great quantities to be shared by and to help define whole sub-cultures. Take fish and chips, the dish of the working class. Its rapid spread throughout the country can be traced back to the flourishing fish trade within Britain and the improving transport links—a national success story. At the turn of the twentieth century, there were already some twenty-five thousand shops, mostly small family businesses, devoted solely to making and selling fish and chips.

Like so many "national" dishes, however, the recipe for the British workers' new meal of choice had its roots in a cultural exchange. Jewish immigrants from Portugal and Spain brought fried fish to the island, while the Brits have the French or the Belgians to thank for their chips. We can no longer determine who exactly first brought the two elements together, but in the 1860s, the dish was already experiencing success in the working-class districts of London and in Lancashire in the North. The salty-sour addition of vinegar was the wild breath of the Atlantic, which the railways carried with them overnight, along with tons of well-chilled fish, from the coast and into the city. The batter gently caresses the fish; take a bite and the hot air trapped in the fluffy outer layer escapes. The white flesh collapses into soft flakes of fragrant meat. Then there are the chips—their tangy grease still on your lips hours later.

Of course, the Brits already had a national specialty, afternoon tea, as a means of identifying a proud kingdom. Teacups in hand, they bore their reputation as the most dignified people in the world as far as their numerous colonies. But even though the lower classes could by now afford the imperial drink, the ritual of afternoon tea belonged to the upper classes who had sufficient leisure time to devote to such comforts. The average factory worker could hardly sit down to tea and scones of an afternoon, nor satisfy their hunger with a dish that was not particularly filling. But fried fish and crispy potatoes? Now there was a proper, tasty, cheap meal, and it immediately captured the hearts of those who would one day rebel against the aristocracy, with its ossified rites and conventions, its delicate teacups and dainty scones.

And so, during both world wars, when practically everything was rationed by the British Ministry of Food—eggs, sugar, jam, meat—the supply of fish and chips was never interrupted, despite massive increases in the price of fish. There were most likely serious fears as to what curbs on fish and chips might mean for national morale. The dish was carted to evacuees in the countryside in special delivery vans, and even the troops in the war zones were supplied with their favorite meal. It was there, amidst trenches and front lines on vast battlefields, that fish and chips experienced their peak as an identity-building national dish. The dish became a lifesaver, and not just because it was so filling. British soldiers used the beloved meal as code to ascertain who was a friend in a foreign place. If a British unit encountered unfamiliar troops abroad, the cry of "Fish!" would soon ring out over the barren landscape. A brief silence. The soldiers would listen, anxiously, and then, to their relief, there would come the reply: "Chips!"

Dishes Named after Bismarck
German Empire

It's the golden age of the German Empire, defined by cities growing at a dizzying pace, temple-like warehouses, colonial stores permeated by the subtle fragrance of coffee and chocolate, Prussian military zeal, and the shining myth of the empire's foundation. Chancellor Otto von Bismarck is a universally revered leading light in this era, a hulk of a man with a striking moustache and a penchant for substantial meals. As is common practice for modern hero worship, during the peak of the cult of Bismarck, everything possible was named after him: a dye, a group of islands in the South Pacific, soaps, ships—and lots and lots of dishes.

The dishes honored, unprompted, with the stateman's name were probably loosely connected to Bismarck's own culinary preferences. They were united by a certain fearlessness when it came to dealing with difficult ingredients, which was typical of nineteenth century cuisine (ultimately, "fat is fuel for the body's machine," as Hedwig Heyl wrote in her 1888 book *ABC der Küche*, or *The ABCs of Cookery*),[25] as well as an honest, deeply German masculinity. A good example of this is the "Bismarck oak"—a Swiss roll covered with buttercream colored brown using cocoa and other ingredients such as pistachios or candied citrus peel, to give it the appearance of a gnarled, moss-covered oak (a symbol of Germany); pieces of its felled trunk would decorate confectionery shops.

There was also the invention of the "alla Bismarck" style of preparation, now more familiar in Italian cuisine, which simply referred to the practice of topping a steak or fillet with a fried egg. Then there was the much more elaborate "sole filets à la Bismarck." The filets would be filled with truffled minced fish, oysters, mussels, and crab tails and, to finish, the dish would be doused with a light mixture of white wine sauce and hollandaise. Of these creations paying homage to the Iron Chancellor, the only one to have stuck in the collective memory is the pickled "Bismarck herring," a dish that makes even the most disastrous night of drinking forgettable come the morning.

The nineteenth century was teeming with these kinds of culinary odes to victorious regents and statesmen. You need only recall *poulet marengo*, named after one of Napoleon's victories, and puff pastry–wrapped beef Wellington, dedicated to the duke who rode to victory at the Battle of Waterloo. Both dishes, much like the "à la Bismarck" creations, were the subjects of somewhat fanciful anecdotes. It is not at all clear how true these stories are, but they were superb hooks for the Prussian art of conversation, carried out night after night at the tables of aristocrats and the bourgeoisie. According to one legend, "beef" Wellington was first served on the battlefield immediately after the victory, made with the flesh of the horses on which the French had ridden to catastrophe. One can easily imagine a Prussian officer listening to this story and gleefully demanding a second helping of victory beef.

Naming dishes after political idols is an intentional act of cultural consolidation and myth-making. By preparing, serving, and ultimately eating sole à la Bismarck, a person grows closer to their hero—through their stomach.

Around 1880, recipes for dishes named after Bismarck were captured in writing and accepted into cookery books, which were increasingly aimed at civil society and not exclusively at professional court chefs, as had previously been the case. One particularly illustrious milestone in this transition was Johann Rottenhöfer's cookbook, first published in 1858. Rottenhöfer was Royal Chamberlain at Wittelsbach Court in Munich, and expressly addressed both courtly cooks and middle-class housewives with his instructions for fine cooking. However, it is doubtful whether his ridiculous patisserie recipes, such as one that instructs the reader in how to create a complete Arc de Triomphe out of hard, sweet dough and roasted almonds, found their way into the kitchens of Munich's rented apartments.

Hedwig Heyl was not quite so exalted as Rottenhöfer, but her work also offered up a stream of opulent and technically demanding dishes. Her book of over eight hundred pages brim with recipes for pies, wild game dishes, seafood, and even ice cream. (Thought was also given to dishes to be served at a person's sickbed: red wine soup, warm Cognac milk, and pureed calf's brain are bound to do bedbound patients a world of good.) Above all, however, she premises her collection of recipes with an introduction that elevates the running of a civil household to the level of a demanding job, incorporating the latest achievements in science and technology. The food of the masses asserted a new self-assurance, and its boundaries with fine cuisine grew hazier by degrees. With Bismarck herring for breakfast and *poulet marengo* for dinner, the people slowly but surely took the bread out of the aristocracy's mouths.

Hunger Strike
Russian Empire

Humanity's relationship with food is deeply ambivalent. Aside from shelter, food and drink are the only things a human body needs for survival, and yet unlike breathing or keeping its heart beating, it cannot satisfy these needs automatically. Food must constantly be obtained and ingested. For millennia, human beings learned this fact the hard way when the harvests failed, when supply routes were hit by war, or when they were simply too poor to buy food. For a person who goes hungry involuntarily, food becomes a hopelessly coveted prize.

For the luckier ones, food is pleasure, physical gratification, and passion. Food fills them up, completing their bodies. It conjures up memories and builds community. Yet it is also a sin and temptation—those who have access to food and still succeed in regulating their consumption demonstrate self-discipline. A person who takes it a step further and goes hungry by choice, cutting off their body from any kind of sustenance, does something radical, something that can be pathological but also political. "We're the last generation who can avert the catastrophe of irreversible climate breakdown. That's why we're going on an indefinite hunger strike," the climate action group *Die Letzte Generation*, or the Last Generation, declared in 2021. Publicly announcing hunger strikes, conscious starvation, has become a weapon in the arsenal of political activism.

One of the first hunger strikes deployed as a political act took place in a Siberian prison. The year was 1882. Several political prisoners had been locked up in tiny cells by the tsarist regime, in such undignified conditions that they began a *golodofka*—a Russian term that the American explorer George Kennan translated as "hunger strike," introducing the phrase to the world. Kennan visited the hunger-striking inmates at their request. He wrote internationally acclaimed reportage and books about his travels through Russia and was particularly interested in the local prison camp, making him the perfect mouthpiece, without whom a protest of this kind would hardly have had any effect. In his notes, Kennan writes:

> I have never been able to understand why a government that is capable when irritated of treating prisoners in this way should hesitate a moment about letting them die, and thus getting rid of them. However, I believe it is a fact that in every case where political hunger-strikers have had courage and nerve enough to starve themselves to the point of death the authorities have manifested

anxiety and have ultimately yielded. It is one of many
similar inconsistencies in Russian penal administration.
[. . .] It shrinks from allowing political convicts to die of
self-starvation and yet it puts them to a slow death in the
"stone bags" of the castle of Schlusselburg.[26]

In doing so, he identifies the Achilles' heel, the vulnerable
spot in every hunger strike: Voluntary starvation is only an
effective protest when those at whom the protest is aimed
care to some degree about the well-being of those on strike.

Societal perception of hunger changed radically
around the turn of the twentieth century. Thanks to the
innovations in the era of industrialization, the problem
of hunger had—at least, in theory—been solved in large
parts of the world. Previously, hunger had generally been
interpreted as a punishment from God or as the failure of
individual people. Now, hunger became a social matter.
From this point onward, hunger in poorer nations was a
humanitarian problem, and in industrialized countries,
it was now the responsibility of the state to ensure its citizens were supplied with food. For this reason, hunger
strikes worked only in countries whose inhabitants had
the choice of not going hungry, or in countries, such as
India during Gandhi's time, which had been colonized by
a wealthy global power.

Food became politicized. Every activist who refused
food was presenting the state with a dilemma. It could not
just let its citizens starve. (Force-feeding via a nasogastric
tube was the first, less than empathetic solution to this
problem, and continued to be practiced until the 1970s

before being outlawed as cruel and inhumane.) In countries where people indulge in good food, are able to choose from long shelves full of delicacies, and enjoy spending time in sublime restaurants, the decision to voluntarily forgo food prompts a kind of incredulous admiration. Not eating becomes a kind of martyrdom. And political martyrs always spell tremendous trouble for heads of state.

The suffragettes of the early twentieth century were regularly arrested in their fight for women's rights and were the next to harness the practices of the tsarist prisoners. The Scottish writer, artist, and suffragette Marion Wallace Dunlop was the first: After a ninety-one-hour hunger strike, she was released from prison early. Hunger strikes by women's rights activists had an explosive effect. More than anything else, the horrifying depictions of the force-feeding of the women endured attracted international sympathy. And the public found the thought of civilized, tea-drinking ladies starving in British prisons so scandalous, so incompatible with all modern humanitarian values that, time and again, the government was forced to yield to the activists and set them free. In 1929, the Indian revolutionaries Bhagat Singh and Jatindra Nath Das invoked these successful campaigns with their own hunger strikes. Then there were the IRA members, who began a hunger strike in 1981 after some initial concerns that a hunger strike might be too feminine a form of resistance. At first, the image of gaunt, martyred bodies seemed too closely tied up with the suffragettes. However, the Irish nationalists soon found their own approach: Fasting martyrs and suffering bodies were, ultimately, deeply Catholic themes.

The politically motivated avoidance of food became a global phenomenon. Mahatma Gandhi viewed his numerous hunger strikes as part of the satyagraha concept of living that he practiced, which focused on a search for truth and nonviolence. There were many facets to Gandhi's determination not to eat. Alongside significant campaigns of fasting, he also practiced a strict asceticism, eating almost nothing but raw, unseasoned dishes. In doing so, he completely ignored the tempting, pleasurable aspect of food—the taste you surrender yourself to, always wanting more. By shutting off this form of pleasure, Gandhi regained control over his being, something explicitly political. Resistance through hunger striking really meant resisting—resisting even the body's most basic urges in order to make a point.

Romanian Caviar and Filet de Boeuf à la Jardinière
Between Paris and Constantinople

It's nighttime. Passengers are lying in soft beds, tucked up tight under silken sheets. A faint scent of polish and leather hangs in the air. Light falls in brief snatches, flickering a little over the tapestries on the walls, illuminating an armchair covered in Genoese velvet. A long sweeping mark shows where the soft fabric has been stroked against the grain by the hands of wide-eyed passengers traveling aboard for the first time. Some lie awake in their beds, listening to the monotonous rattling and puffing below, the steady jolting of the tracks. The Orient Express is making its maiden voyage from Paris to Constantinople, considered by many Western travelers to be the gateway to an Orientalist dream (though the last section of the route involves a ferry and a switch to a different train as the track for the whole route has yet to be completed).

The following evening, a gong calls the passengers for *le dîner*. The travelers have had a pleasant day enjoying bountiful meals, chitchatting over tea, reading newspapers in the library, and having a smoke in the privacy of their own compartments. Dinner is a high point. In the dining car, four-armed gas lamps hang from a ceiling adorned with sumptuous, tropical wood. The tables are laid with cloths of thick, white fabric, silver cutlery, gold-rimmed china, and polished crystal glasses. These are massive and heavy to keep them from slipping off the table if the train jolts suddenly. On the maiden voyage, a ten-course menu is served, though for the train's following journeys, diners would still take their seats before the tempting sight of a several-course culinary experience.

The *Compagnie Internationale des Wagons-Lits*, which operated the Orient Express, had very clear rules for how dishes must be presented and served. The hors d'oeuvres were not to be plated up more than a quarter of an hour before serving, to prevent them from losing their appetizing appearance. Fish was always to be brought to the table whole. When dressing large pieces of meat, the entire joint had to be brought to the table to give "an impression of richness." For *le dîner*, waiters were obliged to wear blue tailcoats and white gloves. The food was part of a careful and elaborate performance that made the sound of juddering rails fade quietly into the background.

Sumptuously furnished ocean liners, luxurious trains: In the nineteenth century, people were traveling faster than ever before and in unprecedented elegance. Jules

Verne was undoubtedly the great storyteller of this cozy age, capturing its opulence in his science fiction. His *Voyages Extraordinaires* emerged from the same grand world as the Orient Express. In Verne's works, three men (and two dogs) hurtle their way to the moon in a projectile, inside of which is a comfortably furnished room with upholstered walls, wraparound sofas, and a gas stove that they use to heat their meat broth. They share a couple of glasses of the best French wine while enjoying the view of the moon's alien landscape. Yet the most outlandish furnishings in Verne's writing could be found twenty thousand leagues under the sea in the Nautilus, a submarine resembling a deep-sea manor house. Diners would sit down to eat in the grand dining room, whose huge oak furnishings, tin-glazed pottery, silk wallpaper and paintings, and table decked with fine china and silver cutlery would be equally as at home in a Parisian townhouse. (To eat, there would be a filet of sea turtle and dolphin liver; Captain Nemo would slay the "water game" himself with a harpoon during his dives.) In the library, with its copper-plated rosewood bookshelves, our hero and his guests observe an eerie giant squid out of a panoramic window framed by pretty draped curtains.

But back to reality—although this scene could just as easily belong to a magical adventure story. The Orient Express is now serving dishes that its wealthy guests are already familiar with from dining at the best restaurants in Europe. The dishes serve as a marker for a certain sophisticated lifestyle. There are oysters, foie gras, and lobsters.

Then the main course, filet de boeuf à la jardinière, is brought out. The waiters present the platters of tender meat with white-gloved hands, cooked to perfection in the galley's coal-fired oven. These are accompanied by a colorful vegetable garnish, the vegetables cut into sticks with precision and artfully arranged. The unfamiliar surroundings slipping past beyond the train's windows serve as the inspiration for other dishes, making it possible to consume the sometimes dangerous-seeming foreign expanse outside in bite-size pieces. (Before embarking on the journey, passengers of the Orient Express were always advised to carry a weapon, as train robberies were a real possibility once the train crossed the Austro-Hungarian border.) On board the Orient Express, a delicacy pertaining to each country the train passes through is served: sturgeon from the Danube, Romanian caviar, and—once the train has arrived in Turkey—a gently steaming heap of cumin-scented pilaf. Yet aside from the food, the rest of this Wild East of sorts remains at a comfortable distance as passengers hurtle along through the landscape at the blistering speed of sixty miles an hour, snug in their elegant railroad cocoon.

Never before had people had to cope with so many technological innovations, so many changes to their everyday lives. The hominess evoked by pretty things and good food in this state-of-the-art train served in part as reassurance. The familiar, trusted ambience—the sedating magic of rosewood and damask napkins—disguised an unleashed technology. The notion of food as pacification also brings to mind those travelers to the moon, who just a hundred years later, would be on their way into space, hoping more than anything that their plastic baggies of dehydrated astronaut food contained familiar dishes like chicken soup and spaghetti Bolognese to keep them grounded during their zero-gravity stay.

Yet the plush comfort and exquisite menus of the Orient Express were not just pure nostalgia, though it might seem so to our contemporary eyes. Like the Nautilus, with a giant squid drifting past its panoramic windows and its own on-board mussel museum, where the uncanny world outside gleamed prettily, rendered harmless, the Orient Express denoted triumphant conquest, the victory of civilized elegance, and the absolute superiority of modern man.

Of course, we know that the protection offered by this blend of visionary innovation and excessive accoutrements was only psychological. There is perhaps no better illustration of this than the nightmarish end of the *Titanic*, the ocean liner born of human hubris, its cozy tapestry of lovely things suddenly, brutally torn apart by an iceberg before the scene descended into a picture of doom calling to mind the End Times. And just moments beforehand, guests on board had been dining on oysters, foie gras, and filet of beef.

Pastrami Sandwich
USA

In Roald Dahl's short story *Pig*, a young boy, born in New York City, is orphaned as a baby and taken into the care of his old, eccentric aunt. His aunt leads a solitary life in a little house at the foot of the Blue Ridge Mountains. She is a strict vegetarian and tells the boy, in no uncertain terms, that meat is disgusting. The boy develops into a brilliant, visionary vegetarian cook. By just ten years of age, he is serving up chestnut soufflé, hominy cutlets, dandelion omelet, and flaming spruce-needle tart. When he is seventeen, his aunt dies unexpectedly. The unworldly boy is forced to travel back to the city. Once he arrives, he stops for a bite to eat at a little restaurant somewhere in Manhattan. He's served the only dish that the grubby little kitchen still has in stock: pork sausages and cabbage. The boy takes a bite and is completely beside himself. It's the best thing he's ever tasted! The waiter takes the boy to the chef. When the boy asks what exactly it is that he has just eaten, the chef replies slyly that it was probably pig—but you can never know for sure because meat is always delivered straight from the slaughterhouse. He tells the boy that he would be welcome to visit. Shortly after, the boy finds himself standing in the yard of a huge brick building, a heavy, sweet scent in the air. He watches as the pigs have a chain looped around their legs, before being pulled into the air by a moving cable and slipping out of sight. The boy then finds a chain around *his* ankle and the machine hauls him upward. He rises higher and higher, chained to the moving cable, screaming in panic, until he finds himself right in front of the slaughterman, who greets him cheerfully before slicing through the boy's carotid artery. The story ends with the sight of a gigantic cauldron full of boiling water, into which the bleeding pigs are summarily dunked.

Dahl's short story initially leaves you feeling somewhat puzzled by its absurd brutality. And yet it identifies several issues that meat-eating societies are repeatedly confronted with (at least when they are open to critical debate). First of all, what actually is the meat that comes from slaughterhouses? It doesn't have to be human flesh, but the stuff we pick out of the refrigerators at the supermarket—those pale pink, marbled rectangles neatly wrapped in cellophane—is visually and emotionally detached from the living being that was killed for it. "It's not death that's eerie, it's the fact that it becomes invisible in a factory," writes Christian Kassung.[27] The moment in which an animal becomes meat remains a blind spot for most people.

The rapidly growing population in the nineteenth century saw meat consumption explode. Far and wide, monstrous factories were shooting up out of the ground, filled with hordes of trudging workers, and at this time, people were convinced that factory workers needed to eat lots of meat to be able to function properly—like a machine running on fuel. And so, society needed more meat, *cheap* meat that was processed into canned products, stock cubes, meat extracts—as much protein and fat as possible squeezed into tiny packages for people who didn't have time to cook. It was the beginning of livestock farming on a huge scale, of enormous slaughterhouses and industrial meat processing.

The catastrophic consequences this had for animal welfare led to the birth of organized animal protection. The United Kingdom blazed the trail in this regard and passed the first animal protection laws in 1822, safeguarding horses, sheep, and heavy livestock against abuse. Increasing numbers of organizations were founded to campaign against animal suffering. For the first time, the people of the new industrialized world felt they had a duty to the animals they ate.

Yet for some communities, this was nothing new. The practice of slaughter anchored in the millennia-old traditions of Judaism, for example, revolves around respect for the animal, as well as hygiene. Judaism permits animals to be killed only according to the method of *shechita*; this requires a single cut that severs the esophagus and the trachea in one continuous movement so that the animal immediately loses consciousness. The knife used must be perfectly sharp and the butcher, the *shochet*, must have studied under a rabbi. Jews were slaughtering livestock in this way during the many centuries when animals were otherwise simply being beaten, stoned, stabbed, or drowned.

Even around 1900, when it had theoretically long been the law that pigs must be stunned before slaughter, this was not always the case in practice. Attempts to facilitate mass slaughter by using machines to stun the animals instantly and painlessly had not yet been successful, and large slaughterhouses were still resorting to using a cudgel, which not all slaughtermen were especially adept with. (The quickest possible way to stun an animal is a crucial point to which debates on respectful slaughter return again and again.)

Let's return to New York. At the turn of the twentieth century, around 30 percent of the city's inhabitants were Jewish. Around half of the butcher's shops were run by Jewish butchers. On the Lower East Side, Jewish bookshops sat snugly alongside kosher bakeries and restaurants. And a culture of conscious meat-eating thrived in family establishments such as Katz's Delicatessen, which exists to this day. Keeping kosher meant that the meat, such as pastrami, served in Jewish establishments had to pass an exceptional number of checks. Pastrami slices would be carefully sliced from the breast or the shoulder of ritually slaughtered cows. The meat would be cured in a spicy, peppery brine, infused with intensely flavored spices like cloves and nutmeg, and then smoked. The red, wafer-thin slices looked like delicate fabric on the plate.

But even the classic Sunday roast enjoyed by non-Jewish families stood for a completely different kind of meat-eating than that of consuming the concentrated extracts from mass cattle farming. The roast, eaten on the one free day of the week, was prepared with care, from a special joint purchased from the butcher.

And so, the birth of industrial slaughterhouses created a new divide between the forms of meat consumption; the thoughtful consumption of higher quality meat versus the thoughtless continual proliferation of cheap meat. Yet the fact remained that a living animal had to be killed to yield this meat, and that this act, hidden behind factory walls, was now cloaked in a kind of gentle forgetfulness. Such is the eternal polarity of meat-eating societies.

c. 1900 CE

Kleiner Schwarzer
Austro-Hungarian Empire

In Vienna, coffee is boiled, not brewed. Coffeehouses roast the beans themselves and each has its own secret blend. Finely ground, like black dust, the coffee is tipped into simmering water and boiled, its fragrance filling the room. The hot coffee is then poured into porcelain coffee pots that have been sitting in a steaming bath of hot water while they wait to be filled. The head waiter strides over to the customer, who has just arrived and taken a seat at one of the round marble tables. The waiter, a combination of a butler and the lord of the manor, greets the customer graciously and offers up a few pleasantries, his black bow tie standing out against his starched white shirt like a silhouette. He then presents the customer with a color palette featuring every possible shade of brown: an almost transparent beige, a warm caramel, several nuttier shades, and a deep, bottomless black. The customer indicates his desired color and the waiter withdraws.

A lowlier waiter brings out the steaming drink, the china cup enthroned on a delicate silver tray with the correct ratio of coffee to milk, and sugar on the side. Next to it is a glass of clear Viennese mountain spring water. The diner is then left in peace. He sinks contentedly behind a rustling wall of newspaper that separates him and his wandering thoughts from the other customers.

"People who sit in coffeehouses want to be alone, but they need company to do it," writes columnist and critic Alfred Polgar.[28] Viennese coffeehouses are a microcosm of modern existence, striving for isolation and individuality while the crowd of people around you grows ever denser. Coffee creates a community of loners. Food is also consumed in coffeehouses, but not as part of big social meals. Coffeehouses offer snacks or light dishes: sausages or a couple of eggs in a cup, into which you plunge a little spoon, the insides soft as butter; pretzel sticks, bread rolls, brioche, or butter *kipferl* to tear into with one hand while the other grips the unwieldy holder clamped around your newspaper. By the end of the nineteenth century, customers at confectioner's shops were indulging in cakes and sweet pastries, and in the coffeehouses, the coffee was flowing like time itself.

Coffee sloshed its way over to Austria from Turkey all the way back in the seventeenth century. People had been drinking it on the Arabian Peninsula since the mid-fifteenth century, and the Ottoman Empire followed suit shortly after. There were three things that made the Viennese coffeehouse into an institution, with its heyday in the fin de siècle. The first was billiards, initially in the form of enormous game tables that were firmly screwed to the floor and that sounded a little bell when the ball fell into the hole. The second was the fact that, unlike strong Turkish coffee, coffee in Vienna required that you remove the dregs after boiling and add milk and sugar. There was something convivial in the embrace of that sweet mild flavor that clearly suited the Viennese better. Yet the real recipe for success—and the third factor at play—was the fact that the international newspapers were laid out, hot off the presses, for patrons to read. They bestrewed chairs, tables, and coat racks like sleepy paper cats. Diners would sit for hours over their newspapers, mute and unmoving, coffee cups cradled between fingers gray with newspaper print, losing themselves in the news and stories of what was happening in the world outside.

But innovation was taking place in the coffeehouse during this time, too; it was the era of the birth of industrial design. The Thonet brothers invented the No. 14 chair, its back composed of two graceful, curving wooden arches, made possible by the new bentwood technique. The epitome of the elegant bistro chair, it soon found its way into every coffeehouse. It could be dismantled into six pieces, saving space during transportation, and reassembled anywhere. Produced en masse, the chair began popping up in Paris bistros and in all the coffeehouses that were emerging across the empire, following the Viennese example. And so, in any town within the Austro-Hungarian Empire, you could find yourself in a Viennese coffeehouse packed with Thonet chairs and marble tables, stepping into coffee-scented scenes like a traveler between worlds—perhaps slipping through one of the enormous mirrors with golden Rococo curlicues—to pass a couple of hours imagining you could hear the rattle of elegant carriages on Vienna's *Ringstrasse* just beyond the paneled walls. Beyond the rim of a coffee cup, a world of imagination began.

The No. 14 chair is intended for brief sips from a *Wiener Melange* (a coffee drink similar to a mild cappuccino), not full meals. It is light and portable, lending itself perfectly to being picked up in a hurry and moved from table to table. A coffeehouse is always in motion. In nineteenth-century Vienna, a businessman would request that business acquaintances and colleagues meet at "his" coffeehouse—holding discussions at the office was deemed rather showy. But it was bohemianism that created its very own world at the coffeehouse, full of talking, arguing, observing. The Viennese coffeehouse litterateur was a regular fixture; at the turn of the century, great names were busy scribbling away at Vienna's marble-topped tables: Karl Kraus, Hermann Bahr, Arthur Schnitzler, Hugo von Hofmannsthal, Franz Werfel, Joseph Roth, Robert Musil, Egon Friedell. A *Kleiner Schwarzer* was your ticket to spending the whole day at the coffeehouse. These writers' work is often characterized by the restless rhythm of doors opening constantly, diners walking around, conversations, the comings and goings of familiar faces and strangers, the cry of "Excuse me, waiter!" The poet Peter

Altenberg gave the magnificent Café Central, located in Vienna's first district, as his home address on his calling card. Below, he conveys this thrumming Viennese backdrop in the style of a telegram: "Mountain stream water burbling crystal clear between cliff and pine tree permutated into music. The trout, a ravishing predator, light gray with red speckles, lurking, standing, flowing, shooting forward, downward, upward, disappearing. Beautiful blood-thirstiness!"[29]

Eventually, the diner would ease themselves heavily out of their chair. The head waiter would wish them goodbye. The only woman to work in the coffeehouse until the mid-nineteenth century, the cashier, would be seated by the exit, waiting behind a till that gave out a noisy rattle. Sternly, she would count out the handful of coins for the *Kleiner Schwarzer* and the diner would stumble back out into the world. Still, it would soon be evening, and they knew they could stop by again soon.

Turnip Jam
German Empire

World War I was the first of the brutal ruptures witnessed in the twentieth century. In 1917, the Germans became aware of a distinct incongruity. On the one hand, they were engaged in a completely new kind of war, a war of the future, making use of the latest military and particularly communicative technologies. Commanders now gave orders by telephone while sitting hunched over marching plans far from the front, and they would receive news via all possible channels: field telephone, radio, telegraph. The words "Watch out—the enemy is listening!" could now be found etched onto every military telephone, constantly reminding callers of the difficult-to-grasp but sinister threat of telecommunications surveillance. They found themselves at the heart of the first modern media war.

The year 1917 also revealed something that had been known since time immemorial: that people cannot exist without sufficient supplies, and that these provisions can be interrupted quicker than anyone would like to imagine. Whether due to bad decisions, bad luck with the weather, or unfathomable administrative chaos, supply chain interruptions ensured that people would very suddenly find themselves subject to living standards they believed industrialization had banished forever.

The German Empire lurched ecstatically into an apocalyptic war without any supplies to speak of. Prior to the outbreak of the war, the Germans had been feeding their pigs, which were in abundant supply, with barley from Russia, who was now the enemy. Without Russian barley, the pigs would now have to be fed more potatoes, which were also in limited supply. Since the pigs would soon be without adequate food and other provisions were dwindling, the Imperial Statistical Office calculated that they should slaughter the five million pigs and preserve the meat in cans. (The statisticians' calculations were based on figures that were partially incorrect; farmers provided the Office with underestimates of their potato harvests out of a fear that they would be forced to give up their precious potatoes for the fatherland.) But since all of Germany's metal was required to manufacture arms, the only cans available were made of low-quality materials. A large portion of the pork stores spoiled, and new livestock was in short supply following the mass slaughter. Then there was no manure for the potatoes; manure was usually imported from Chile, but it could no longer get through due to the British naval blockade. Worse still, in the autumn of 1916 the rain was endless. The few potatoes that did grow rotted in the wet soil. The final straw saw the state's completely immobilized bureaucratic machinery sporadically distribute the few supplies that did arrive from allied and occupied nations, leaving its citizens desperate for a reliable source of homegrown food.

In the end, the country was left with a single food product that was easy to cultivate, grew across the land, and was, consequently, available to all. It was rich in vitamins, if rather low in calories. Generally thought of as food for pigs, it stank when cooked, with a flavor ranging from bitter to repellent. Nobody wanted to eat it, and yet it was the only thing that might save them from starvation. It was the turnip.

"Only when the appropriate treatment of turnips has gained ground among the civic population will the mistrust with which this vegetable has hitherto been regarded gradually recede," claimed government posters distributed across cities in the late autumn of 1916. These were followed by a number of clarifications regarding failed potato harvests. It's no small irony that, 150 years before, no one in the country had wanted to eat potatoes until famine led to the population abruptly changing its opinion. Now all people wanted was potatoes, not turnips. And so, the country went hungry once again. Government posters continued: "It is now therefore necessary to place turnips, which will later decay badly and lose their pleasant flavor, in the service of the sustenance of the nation. They must be pickled and dried so that they keep for the early months of spring." Another hopeful rallying cry to finish: "Germany's valiant housewives will not fail in this regard."

This rather unpromising situation released a wealth of ideas, as countless cookery books from the period demonstrate. If there's nothing to eat but stinky turnips, the thinking went, then we can at least come up with an infinite number of ways to prepare them. This scarcity served as a catalyst for a diversity of recipes that, at times, bordered on absurd.

As well as pickles and dried turnips, the root can be used in soups, salads, fritters, dumplings, casseroles, and even candies. Or simply combine soft, cooked turnip with sauerkraut—the latter is just grated turnips that have sat around in vinegar for a while—and, voilà, you've got a vegan dish made with local produce, with two different textures. At lunchtime, children were munching turnips instead of sandwiches. Turnip soup for breakfast, turnip steak for lunch, and turnip cake for dinner. You could also grate turnips, dry them in the oven, grind them in a coffee grinder, and you had—yes, you've guessed it—coffee, of a sort. You could even leave some dried turnip unground and smoke it in your pipe.

And while the turnips were stewing in the oven, simmering on the stove, and coming to the boil in the coffee pot, you could put four pounds of turnips, three pounds of raisins, and one lemon—if you had one—through the meat grinder and then boil the mixture with sugar and water to make jam. "The jam can be improved by adding fruit juice," advises the recipe's unknown author, touching on what is perhaps the root's best feature: Turnips take on the flavor of the other ingredients during cooking or preserving. Cook them with a few apples and you get a large quantity of apple puree. Cook them with celery or carrots and they will help to stretch them out. The common turnip works wonders when it comes to culinary imitation. And yet the nation's Turnip Winter will be remembered by millions of Germans as a time of trauma.

And in less than thirty years' time, the same musty fug of turnips would again permeate the corridors of bombed-out homes and bring that trauma back to the forefront of people's minds. Food can be a catalyst for painful memories, too.

Student Meals
Weimar Republic

"[This building] has been used as a canteen since 1922. It would have been more than sufficient for requirements at the time. Today, we can make the claim of having the oldest and the worst canteen in Germany."

These are the opening words from a 1959 letter petitioning the German Interior Minister on behalf of the students of Georg-August University in Göttingen, Germany, explaining the unacceptable conditions of the university canteen. Despite a student population that had grown to almost 2,700 students, there was only space for 350. "Long queues of hungry students form outside the building and in the dining hall itself . . ." And "the working conditions of the unfortunate women who spend every day—including Sundays—in the cellar peeling 20–30 hundredweights of potatoes undoubtedly require no further comment." After further gruesome descriptions of the canteen's conditions, the author declares, "The huge numbers of meals required are beyond manageable. Constant special efforts, overtime and a lot of luck are required for any catering to enjoy some degree of success. The food is often criticized by the students regardless, along with the rooms in which they are to eat it. The criticism is entirely justified."[30]

Students have always been thought of as a group with very little money, who therefore deserve support. It was for this reason that, well into the 1920s, Germany had what were known as *Freitische*, or "free tables." These were seats at literal tables—in community centers, restaurants, or even wealthy families' dining rooms—which were sponsored by foundations or private benefactors, where lucky students could regularly enjoy a free meal. This ensured that students did not have to expend their mental faculties worrying about food. Then came the *Mensa*, or canteen, in 1922; Göttingen's was the first, a space where students were not only able to enjoy affordable food but where they could also relax and mix within their academic community. The *Stammessen* was a fixed, nutritious menu comprising soup, main, and dessert; the exact composition of the meal was a constant topic of debate. Following the two World Wars, many students who had often been on the front needed feeding up to combat the effects of severe malnourishment and starvation as well as serious illnesses. The *Mensa* often served as a kind of heated day room during this time. Later, student services—who were responsible for the health of the students—focused heavily on the fact that students usually engaged in highly demanding mental activity while doing relatively little physical exercise. How, they wondered, could you feed students' minds without overburdening their stomachs?

The *Mensa* acted like a seismograph, gauging social and political tremors within the student body. As such, the letter to the Interior Minister was no mere list of nagging gripes about the lack of dining spaces. It was testament to a group that was becoming increasingly politicized. In Göttingen, students were moving in an increasingly left-thinking direction from a strictly conservative starting position, becoming ever more critical and active. The students of Göttingen were developing a mind-set that prevented them from tolerating the slightest inconvenience—such as the poor quality of the food in their canteen.

In the 1960s, Germany's university canteens were rebuilt and reformed to better serve the rapidly growing number of students. The *Mensa* was increasingly developing into a colossus of communal catering only made possible thanks to automation; conveyor belts and machines for peeling and chopping were put to use preparing the untold quantities of potatoes and vegetables required to feed hungry students. While the fifties were characterized by canteens with white tablecloths and waiters in uniform, now, it was all about self-service and functionality. However, the notion of the *Mensa* as a mass operation, a mere "feeding station," was to be avoided at all costs; many of the new hall-like canteens were fitted with dividing walls to make the individual spaces smaller and less factory-like. In the late sixties and early seventies, protests and unrest were the order of the day. Reacting to the general unrest, the newly founded University of Bremen consulted the psychoanalyst Alexander Mitscherlich about what they could do better. Mitscherlich envisioned a canteen as a hierarchy-free space, an idealized campus in which all members of the university could meet as equals, always open to spontaneous, interdisciplinary exchange. What's more—and this was practically revolutionary—the insular academic community was to be split open and use of the *Mensa* extended to non-members of the university. Here was another case of conservative values being dropped in favor of anti-authoritarian democratization. Again, food was at the center of the reflections and controversies of a community, coming together time and again around the same table.

The history of the *Mensa* canteens and their food reveals the politicization of the academic community, the formation of its identity, its convictions and trends. In the summer of 1984, the *Mensa* in Augsburg laid on its first "health food week," which included vegetarian dishes. The nineties saw the rise of colorful international themes—serving stations creaked under plates piled with *Café de Paris* chicken filets, "American" pork cutlets, "Chinese" goujons, and "Mexican" rice. By the end of the nineties, there was an "eco menu" comprising locally grown foods. Another environmental campaign flared up in Freiburg in 2016: Several students calling themselves the *Bänderer* gathered around the automatic conveyor belt—or "band," from which the group derived its name—that carried trays of leftover food to the waste disposal. Like culinary salvage workers, they grabbed the plates and ate the leftovers. By doing this, the forty-or-so *Bänderer* hoped to take a stand against food waste. The campaign was soon stopped by student services, who erected walls of partition screens around the conveyor belts, immediately prompting new, heated debate. Tempers ran high . . . and the vegan *chili sin carne* slowly sweated away under the heated gantry.

Bauhaus Canapés and *Carneplastico*
Europe

Whoosh, ding-a-ling—clang! Whoosh, ding-a-ling—clang!
This is the sound of the Bauhaus school in February 1929,
where the Metallic Festival is underway. Another guest,
glued or squeezed inside sheet metal, hurtles down a huge
glittering silver slide into the ballroom: *Whoosh!* Like a
caterpillar in a tubular tinplated cocoon, a Bauhaus student plods down the stairs, which have been fitted with
bells—*ding-a-ling, clang*—searching for a colleague to
tighten a loose screw in her costume. The whole building
shimmers with light reflected off frying pans, spoons—
whatever metallic materials the students have been
able to get their hands on—and caricatures of dancing
avant-gardists glide over curved plate metal.

Partying was a requirement of the artistic synthesis
that lived and breathed in the Bauhaus, the art school
known for its avant-garde approach to design. Even the
food served at these parties could do little to escape the

all-encompassing Bauhaus lifestyle. But these were no middle-class menus. Instead, there were canapés: small square slices of bread topped with repeating layers of cheese and cold cuts, accompanied by small pyramids of remoulade or lentils, all arranged in a geometric design. It was like the Triadic Ballet on little pieces of bread. In the midst of all this floated gingerbread figures made by the master textile artist and weaver, Gunta Stölzl. There was a wiry gingerbread leopard and dancers with wasp-like waists and athletic arms, all animated and lost in a luminous world of fantasy, just like her carpets and textiles.

Not all avant-gardists were as crafty and care-free in the kitchen, though. Italian futurists chose to draft a complete program of political visions for the future rather than whipping up convoluted culinary creations. In December 1930, Filippo Tommaso Marinetti published his *Manifesto della Cucina Futurista*, or *The Manifesto of Futurist Cooking*, prompting fear and horror among Italians. The nationalist-minded Marinetti, they learned, wanted to abolish pasta. He claimed that the Italian national dish would ultimately induce lassitude and pessimism. In fact, the domestic production of pasta dough depended on importing foreign wheat; it would be more patriotic, Marinetti claimed, to support Italian rice production. In the same breath, Marinetti dreamed aloud of opening the kitchen up to chemistry in the hope that chemists might invent a pill capable of providing the human body with sufficient sustenance. Soon, Marinetti argued, radios would even be able to send out waves of nutrition.

Marinetti pulled veritable showstoppers out of his sizzling pot of magical wishful thinking. Shortly after the manifesto was published, the Futurists opened their first restaurant in Turin, *La Taverna del Santopalato*. The food served there meandered between avant-gardist artwork, performance, and sheer lunacy. Take *carneplastico*, a meat sculpture. Promoted pretentiously as a "synthetic interpretation of the Italian landscape," the carneplastico was a cylindrical meat loaf made of roast veal. The meat loaf was filled with eleven different vegetables and topped with a dollop of honey. This would then be placed atop the geometric body of the dish—a ring of sausages—and three golden chicken meatballs would be positioned around the base. Another dish, the "chicken Fiat" served with whipped cream, bordered on inedible: The bird was filled with steel ball bearings and was intended as a tribute to the Fiat factory. And there was a militaristic enthusiasm for technology and the armed forces underlying the "aerofood," which crossed the line entirely into the realm of performance. The diner would be served a plate of black olives, bulb fennel, and kumquats, and would be invited to eat these with their right hand, all the while using their left hand to stroke a "tactile rectangle." A shiver would run up the diner's back as their fingers glided over sandpaper, red silk, and black velvet. A waiter, standing behind, would spritz the diner with essence of carnations. Meanwhile, a mixture of Bach and the roaring sound of an airplane engine would be played from the kitchen at a positively infernal volume. Is it food, or is it art?

In the Bauhaus, food was viewed more as passing or-
namentation than part of an artistic synthesis, while the
Futurists considered it to be a vehicle for their feverish
visions. Three decades later, though still in an avant-
garde vein, the Swiss artist Daniel Spoerri founded *Eat
Art*. Spoerri was interested in taste as an aesthetic experience, which he would then thoroughly deconstruct. In
1970, a whole twenty years before chef Ferran Adrià un-
veiled his pipettes and liquid nitrogen, Spoerri presented
the Banana Trap Dinner. To begin, guests were given turtle soup served in a demitasse, and the meal ended with
coffee served in a soup bowl. It was a clever switch that
scrutinized the relationship between taste and expectations. Does soup taste different when we think we're getting coffee?

A generation later, Kai Söltner, an artist and skilled
chef, took the intellectualization of eating to an unexpected level. At a Dada event, he literally cooked books, in
pots almost as enormous as the uproar he provoked. (The
books, since you're asking, were *Les Chants de Maldoror*
by Lautréamont and Achim Szepanski's *Capitalization:
Vol. 2*.) He then dripped the book soup into vodka. One
valiant gulp later and he had absorbed surrealism's radical
beginnings—in the most literal sense. Cheers!

Food has frequently played a significant role in art. The
Dutch still lifes of the seventeenth century come to mind,
their virtuosity making them a delicious feast for the eyes.
By contrast, avant-garde approaches to the culinary arts
demand something more tangible; you should be able to

taste the aesthetic, even if it doesn't taste all that good. And perhaps chewing and tasting allows us to scratch the surface of the untouchable nature of art, like Picasso, whose cubism emerged in pubs and who was captivated by the simplest objects in the kitchen, which is why he painted them so often; he said, "A spoon for a glass of absinthe [. . .] wine, raw ham, a fattened chicken. This demystification of painting glorifies everyday life and shows the taste of real life."[31]

Langouste Belle Aurore
French Republic

It's evening in Lyon and the room is filled with elegantly dressed people. Chandeliers cast their glow over long tables set with black-and-white checked tablecloths. Waiters in white suits see to it that the glasses that litter the table are constantly filled. The diners look toward the door to the kitchen and their eyes glimmer with anticipation. There, among the white tiles and steamed-up muntin windows, a sturdy woman is tending to huge pots and sauté pans. The air is heavy with the scent of butter and cream. And then, dinner is served: *poularde en demi-deuil*, baby chicken with truffle slices like delicate black crepe under its crispy skin. A gratin of quenelles with poached pike, floating in an unctuous ocean of béchamel sauce, crayfish, butter, and cream. And, of course, *langouste belle aurore*: a whole lobster cooked in cognac and a liter of cream and served in a vol-au-vent, a cylindrical pastry shell. The first guests tuck in, knives crunching through the crisp pastry casing. Flaky, almost transparent crumbs of pastry flutter down into the fragrant sauce. The waiters dart around busily while the diners sink into a satiated food coma.

The cook tending to the bubbling pots of cream is Eugénie Brazier. Her restaurant, *La Mère Brazier*, is one of the first to be awarded three Michelin stars. Her second restaurant on Col de la Luère has also been awarded three Michelin stars, making Brazier not just the first woman but the first person ever to receive six Michelin stars. (A budding cook by the name of Paul Bocuse will soon become her apprentice.)

The Michelin guide's star system is still in its infancy. Famously, the little red guide was thought up by Michelin—a tire manufacturer—in 1900, to provide its customers not just with useful information such as the addresses of auto shops and filling stations but also to offer ideas for where drivers might like to go in their automobiles; if customers were going to wear out their quality Michelin tires, they might as well do so for a good reason. The Michelin brothers were doing pioneering work with their little red booklet almost without realizing. At the turn of the twentieth century, road networks had yet to be fully developed and road signs were few and far between. It was practically impossible to find your way to a remote country inn. The guides were soon kitted out with road maps, which happened to be so good that they were later used by the Allies during World War II to orient themselves in bombed-out France. Michelin covered the country with a fine network of maps, mapping the country's most sophisticated eateries in the process. From 1926, recommended restaurants were highlighted with a star; five years later, Michelin introduced the rankings that endure to this day. The three stars signify the highest possible score—in Michelin's words, *vaut le voyage*—worth a special trip. One star suggests that it's worth stopping in if you're in the area, while two stars means a restaurant is worth a detour. And so, the notion of gourmet tourism, the culinary pilgrimage, was born.

The concept of cooking as art has existed in elite circles since antiquity. When the Michelin guide appeared on the scene, restaurant reviews were already in existence, if somewhat on the fringes. The godfather of the genre, Alexandre Balthazar Laurent Grimod de la Reynière, legendary connoisseur from the Parisian aristocracy, published his *L'Almanach des gourmands* in the early nineteenth century. Yet the introduction of the Michelin star saw the world of award-winning cuisine emerge; the guide provided a clearly systematized rating to which any keen gourmet could refer, fueling whole careers—or finishing them.

Initially, the art of cooking experienced an enhanced appreciation of sorts. A three-star restaurant was suddenly a sensation, attracting celebrities. Charles de Gaulle and Marlene Dietrich came to Lyon to eat Brazier's lobster drowned in cognac cream. More than anything, however, the star system established an approach to food characterized by shoptalk and an increasingly intellectual seriousness. The professional gourmet emerged out of the rustling pages of the Michelin guide and the numerous other gastronomy guides that would follow. Food wasn't about eating your fill; it was about the experience of taste.

The relationship between human beings and food had already come quite far in this respect. From an essential ingredient for preserving human life, the acquisition of which was at the center of human beings' every waking thought, to a means of, in part, cruel social distinction, food had now become an object of critical opinion and evaluation. (Interestingly, it was at this time—not to overemphasize this fact—that new systems for classifying and evaluating art were devised in the art theory of the greats such as Erwin Panofsky and Aby Warburg.) The stars were soon determining who rose and who fell in the world of good taste. Michelin was now sending internationally experienced critics, known as *inspecteurs*, to restaurants where, like secret agents in disguise, they would drop by unannounced to test the food, several times, to determine who was worthy of a new star, who deserved to keep their stars—and who deserved to lose them. Not all chefs could stand the permanent pressure of these seemingly arbitrary visits. Stories of burnout and even suicides grew amid the clusters of stars, and more and more restaurants removed themselves from the pressure of it all by deliberately forgoing assessment or giving their star back. Even so, today, professional cooks cannot escape the judgment of genuine or self-proclaimed restaurant critics. This is the legacy of the first gastronomy guide. A restaurant can shut its doors to the Michelin guide, but all those virtually shared scores, opinions, and reviews on blogs and social media are still out in the world and are often much more harshly worded than a professional review. The Michelin guide was just the—comparably, rather civilized—beginning.

Pan de Muerto and Sugar Skulls
Mexico

On evenings like these, the cemeteries of Mexico are awash with color and life. The gravestones and the paths between the graves are decked out with vibrant yellow and orange flower heads. Garlands and elaborate, gauzy paper lace flutter in the balmy air. A sea of flickering candles bathes everything in a yellow glow. Families sit at the graves—parents, grandparents, children, aunts, uncles—and picnic with their dead loved ones in their final resting places.

The living perch on little chairs or simply squat on the ground. They have brought along great baskets and bags containing their dearly departed's favorite dishes and are busy unpacking them. There are tamales just the way a great uncle liked them, the spicy meat and vegetable filling wrapped in a dough made from corn and lard and then slow-cooked, wrapped in a corn husk. There is also *pan de muerto*, bread of the dead, small, soft, sweet bread buns smelling of aniseed. The buns are topped with two crossed bones made of dough with a ball in the middle, representing bones and a tear, and they are scattered with plenty of sugar. In the days before *Día de los Muertos*, the Day of the Dead, the sweet scent of pan de muerto emanates from kitchens across town, as the round buns and their decorative bones rise gently in the oven. Supermarket shelves and the window displays of *dulcerías* are close to buckling under the weight of countless garishly colored skulls, or *calaveras*, made from icing, amaranth, or chocolate. The skulls are a favorite with children—it's even possible to have the name of a departed loved one written on the skull in icing. And next to the skulls stand battalions of colorful marzipan coffins, like elongated snack bars, studded with delicate crosses.

This relaxed sense of communion with one's dead ancestors is deeply entrenched in Mexican culture, and the Aztecs, Mayans, Mexica, and Totonacas probably also celebrated their dead in this way, beginning over three thousand years ago. However—though, strangely enough, most people these days prefer to ignore this—Día de los Muertos in its current form is likely a twentieth century invention. The sugar skulls, skeletons, and marzipan coffins may have emerged under President Lázaro Cárdenas, who held office from 1934 and took great pains to strengthen Mexico's indigenous identity.

Either way, the tradition of the meal with the dead, the idea of the dead and the living communing over food, is one that humanity has nurtured for thousands of years.

In ancient Rome, it was customary for the family of the departed to gather for a meal at the graveside straight after the burial. Many catacombs and burial chambers were fitted with stone tables or even wrap-around dining benches where the dead person's closest relatives could take a seat. In the ancient Middle East, more than three thousand years ago, ritual meals were eaten in burial chambers; the family would sit on stone benches in the crypt and eat and drink with as much dignity as they could muster alongside the open sarcophagi. In the Levant at this time, everyday life saw great importance placed on tending to the dead. The spirits of ancestors had to be regularly provided with food and drink, and if this duty was neglected, descendants faced the risk of angry ghosts taking revenge by inflicting illness and misfortune on their living relatives. By contrast, in modern-day Sicily, it is the dead who present their descendants with an offering: At the *festa dei morti*, the dead hide little gifts and traditional sweets, such as special almond biscuits, sugar poppets, and colorful marzipan fruit, for children to find. After the treasure hunt, people visit the graves of the generous dead and decorate them with flowers before gathering for a family feast.

Of course, in numerous regions of the world, people continue to gather for a reception that, though it does not tend to take place next to the grave, is very much influenced by the burial that shortly precedes it. Food as a cultural practice for building community seems to be so deeply anchored within human traditions that it can even help us forge closer connections with our dead.

But let's return to Mexico. Alongside the morbid sweets, the Yucatan peninsula boasts another firm custom for the Day of the Dead. People prepare *mukbil pollo*, a huge tamale filled with chicken, pork, garlic, tomatoes, and chiles. This oversize pasty is dunked in a spicy stock until it is fully saturated and then wrapped in banana leaves and baked in a pit in the ground, just as the Mayans once did. Hours later, the mukbil pollo is dug up and carefully unwrapped. The inside glows a reddish orange. It releases a plume of hot scents, spicy, fresh, and familiar all at once. It is a time capsule filled to the brim with the stories of our lives.

It is telling that ancestor worship is often tied to extra special dishes. Be they sugar skulls or pan de muerto, giant tamales or marzipan fruits, these dishes—their flavors, their scents, the way they look—instantly stir up memories. We can imbibe those memories, in a sense, while eating together. And in doing so, we can unite with our dear departed relatives for a time—until dinner is over.

1937 CE

BBC Omelet
United Kingdom

London, 1937. The BBC, still in its experimental phase, puts charming restaurateur Marcel Boulestin in front of the camera and has him cook live on TV. He is the first person ever to prepare food on television. And what does Boulestin make on this historic occasion? An omelet.

To understand why the pioneering days of television saw an omelet enjoy its very own TV premiere, we must take a step back. In 1923, having previously worked in London as an author, decorator, French teacher, and wine consultant, Boulestin penned a much sought-after bestseller, *Simple French Cooking for English Homes*. His success undoubtedly had something to do with the political and economic age during which his books emerged. British cuisine had been on the decline since World War I, when the island nation faced difficulties importing sufficient quantities of food, causing many ingredients to be rationed by the state (efforts to combat the catastrophic consequences continue to this day). At the same time, the middle class was growing, the government was supporting house-building, and people were moving into their own little homes, driving cars, and purchasing new household appliances. People were increasingly interested in being able to make something tasty out of the limited ingredients that were available to them. And that was where Boulestin came in, seizing the moment at just the right time with his approachable French cuisine.

After writing other bestsellers, such as *How to Keep a Good Table for Sixteen Shillings a Week*, Boulestin opened London's most elegant and most expensive restaurant, Restaurant Boulestin, which—being a former interior designer—he decorated with avant-gardist murals and bright brocade curtains. Boulestin was not a trained chef; he was simply a gourmet who had taken it upon himself to convert British palates. Yet now here he was, the first person to cook a dish on television. And, thus, he became the forefather of the TV chef, a dazzling expert/connoisseur/self-promoter, a presenter for a genre of television that placed cooking, rather than eating, front and center as a meaningful social activity—an activity that could, for instance, be undertaken under the relaxed and conversational instruction of a sophisticated Frenchman. And so, quite casually and for the first time, cooking became the subject of its very own media production.

So, omelets. *Tant de bruit pour une omelette*, as the French say—or, "much ado about an omelet." Belying its seeming simplicity, there is an entire culinary canon demonstrating that this dish, comprising just three ingredients, actually *is* worth all that ado. Few of the greats of French cooking have failed to give some thought to the omelet, both before and after its premiere on the BBC: Auguste Escoffier, Paul Bocuse . . . and Jacques Pépin explained that, if he wanted to test a young chef, he would have them cook an omelet; true skill, he explained, revealed itself in things that, on the surface, seemed the simplest.

An omelet connoisseur uses nothing but butter, eggs, and salt. Just a pinch of salt, but lots and lots of the other two ingredients. Alice B. Toklas, Gertrude Stein's life partner, who ran the grande dame's household and wrote numerous cookbooks, shared an omelet recipe from the painter Francis Picabia in one of her books. "The eggs of course," she wrote, "are not scrambled." Instead, mix together eight eggs, salt the mixture, and pour it into a pan. Stir the mixture over the lowest possible flame for half an hour, while very slowly adding half a pound of butter—"not a speck less, more if you can bring yourself to it."[32] The resulting mixture should be silky, Toklas writes, a view shared by Auguste Escoffier, according to whom the omelet must be both smooth and moist at once. When it leaves the pan, folded over like a deliciously scented draped throw, it should still not be quite cooked through, but should finish cooking on the warm plate.

Other than that, the rule of thumb while cooking an omelet is to shake, shake, shake. Around thirty years after Boulestin, by which time television had long been the leading medium of choice, a certain Julia Child shot to fame with her cookery program, *The French Chef*. Once again, the focus of this program was on simple French cooking, though this time American households were the target audience. Like Boulestin before her, Child cooked a French omelet and demonstrated just how she believed an omelet ought to be prepared. With a steadfast grip, she clasped the handle of her non-stick pan and shook it until the mixture came away from the bottom of the pan and folded itself into the desired shape.

Unfortunately, it's not possible to revisit Boulestin's first television appearance to see if he, too, shook the pan with such vigor. In 1937, it was not yet technologically possible to record the cookery program, which was broadcast live. What we do know is that opting for an omelet was a clever choice on Boulestin's part. The ingredients were simple and few in number, and a reasonable degree of technical knowledge was sufficient to follow the recipe. However, the lavish use of butter must have been thrilling for a nation whose cuisine was initially based on dishes covered in heavy pastry or pulled, sizzling, from a deep-fat fryer, to provide the warmth needed on cold, wet days. And, of course, it offered a touch of luxury in hard times, a knowing wink that said, "Go on, treat yourself; who knows how much longer it'll last?"

Boulestin's program, *Cook's Night Out*, ran until 1939. He spent the last years of his life under the German occupation in Paris, where he died before the war ended.

Vegetable Pie
United Kingdom

"Free him of his craving for meaty stews . . . cleanse him completely of his taste for blood," reads the somewhat brutal call in *The Vegetarian*, the newspaper for the Natural Living Society. The year is 1892. Emerging out of an awareness of the cruelty of the new industrial slaughterhouses, this aggressive vegetarianism represented a radical view of nineteenth century meat-heavy cooking. Yet, at the turn of the twentieth century, it still wasn't going far enough for some people.

In 1900, a small group of somewhat eccentric contemporaries attempted to forgo meat, eggs, milk, and all other animal products. Henri Oedenkoven, son of an industrialist, and his lover, Ida Hofmann, established a colony of alternative-minded individuals, intended as a kind of detox institution and located at Monte Verità in a beautiful and remote region of Ticino, Switzerland. Old photographs from this time depict barefoot dancers in loose clothing, as well as trays of provisions consisting of two slices of dry bread, unpeeled fruits, and a heap of nuts. It is perhaps not surprising given this rather stark fare that some guests regularly sneaked down into the village to eat rare steak in secret.

The term "veganism" was invented half a century later by a Brit, Donald Watson. Watson founded the first Vegan Society in Birmingham in 1944. At the time, veganism required renouncing all products that its adherents viewed as perpetrating suffering on other living beings. The first vegans were some way off from discovering that their diet could also lead to an exciting new field of culinary experience. The third edition of the society magazine, *The Vegan*, introduced a column for vegan recipes. Among these first recipes were orange walnut cookies, wholemeal almond biscuits, and a vegetable pie with mashed potato and baked beans. It was simple home cooking without all the ethically questionable ingredients, but it was far from exciting. It would be a long time before vegan cuisine would be able to shake off its reputation for a lack of imagination, as evidenced by this first vegetable pie. The old prejudice that claims vegan food is bland, pleasure-free, and even unpleasantly healthy tasting endures to some degree to this day.

In the decades that followed, however, the arguments for veganism became ever more varied and impassioned, responding to an increase in global problems and also incorporating new scientific insights. Committed animal rights advocates went vegan out of concern for animal welfare. Yet, there were also increasingly compelling medical grounds for a vegan diet. And today, there is a strong tide of veganism within the climate movement, since industrial livestock farming contributes massively to global warming and is hugely damaging to the environment. More than anything, it is the latter that explains why veganism heralds a paradigm shift in the discussion around how and what we eat. This shift ensures that there is a socio-political dimension to every conversation we have about food. Regardless of whether we continue to eat animal products, restrict our consumption of them, or forgo them altogether, each of these attitudes toward food is also a political statement. Henceforth, each individual person's relationship to what they eat is also representative of their relationship to our planet and the great global crisis of our time. We have arrived at an era in which food is completely politicized.

In debates between vegans and carnivores, the latter often argue that eating meat is deeply entrenched in human nature, presumably envisaging the hunter-gatherers of the last Ice Age. But, of course, this is nonsense. If the history of food reveals anything, it is that humans have adapted their diets time and again. From the Neolithic era onward, the majority of Central Europe regularly ate an almost exclusively vegan diet of bread and grain porridge—and that's without even mentioning cultures that are influenced by Buddhism, for instance.

Nevertheless, human beings continue to prove themselves stubborn creatures of habit, requiring time to move away from cultural patterns that have become ingrained over centuries. In Western cultural circles, we are very much entrenched in the tradition of the French-influenced cuisine of the modern era, as well as the cuisine of industrialization. Meat consumption in the nineteenth century, which bordered on insatiable, most likely laid the foundations for today's gastronomic habits. You only need to look at Henriette Davidis's *Praktisches Kochbuch*, or *Practical Cookbook*, a popular wedding gift for prospective young housewives in the nineteenth century. The front section of the book certainly contains vegetable dishes, though all of them are intended solely to serve as side dishes. These are followed by thirty-seven ox and beef recipes, sixty veal recipes, thirty-seven pork recipes, and so on. Then come the egg and milk recipes, and, finally, a whole world of sauces—never without melted butter—which are poured over everything. This animal-product-centric cuisine was still being served up by the middle classes in Western industrialized countries just a few generations ago.

There's also a close link between meat and societal perceptions of masculinity that stems from the age of industrialization. The first contemporary insights into nutritional value and calories led us to believe that men working hard in factories needed as much meat as possible to build muscle and strength, much like high-powered steam engines. The image of a beefcake of a man fed on hearty meat-packed meals still lingers in our minds. In fact, men today eat an average of double the recommended meat allowance. But now that more professional athletes—including those in traditionally "masculine" sports such as soccer and American football—are improving their performance via a vegan diet, will anything change in this regard?

Questions of masculinity aside, the world of high-end gastronomy is currently in the process of discovering plant-based cuisine. Animal-free dishes have become a viable luxury product; 2021 saw the three-Michelin-star restaurant, Eleven Madison Park, become the first to serve up a completely vegan menu. At the restaurant in New York City, you'll find the seeds of kochia scoparia, hand-picked in Japan, cooked in an algae-plankton broth. The menu has also debuted crème fraiche made from fermented almonds, and a delicate tartar made from cucumber, melon, and smoked daikon. Vegan food has come a long way since the days of mashed potatoes and baked bean pies.

Leftovers
Worldwide

The practice of storing food for later is as old as the practices of harvesting, hunting, and cooking. Since human beings have had access to refrigerators, their options have expanded beyond time-proven preservation techniques like pickling and canning. Now, we're able to keep produce fresh and leftovers edible without any further preparation—at least for a few days.

In frugal times such as the postwar years, the dishes that were most ubiquitous were those that made use of leftovers. The last remnants of the Sunday roast could be cooked up in a traditional German *Bauernfrühstück* (a dish of fried potatoes with scrambled egg and bacon), shepherd's pie, or *Hoppelpoppel*, Swedish *pyttipanna*, Danish *biksemad*, or Austrian *Gröstl*. Marrowbones, the leftover carcass from a roast, and leftover scraps of meat could be boiled up to make stock. Bouillabaisse is another classic meal of leftovers, invented by fishmongers in Marseille to use up unsold fish. In Korea, leftover rice, vegetables, and a little meat would be fried up to make bibimbap, and a raw egg would be cracked over the top. And to make ratatouille, simply take whatever vegetables that are lying at the bottom of the fridge, chop them up, and sauté them.

In 1946, an American businessman by the name of Earl Silas Tupper seized on this trend. Several years before, he had become familiar with a new material: polyethylene. Initially, he used it to produce bits and pieces for the military, such as pieces for gas masks. When the war ended, he was one of the first to introduce plastic to the civilian market, presenting his "Wonder Bowl" to the world. These light, almost transparent bowls, in bright or pastel colors, had a patented airtight seal. "Locks in that just-cooked freshness to keep your leftovers fresh for days," proclaims a 1960s advertisement for Tupper's company, Tupperware.

Despite being praised for their lightness and their minimalist design, which was positively futuristic for the 1940s, the Tupperware containers sat untouched on department store shelves. They seemed too strange, like brightly colored aliens in a peaceful world of ceramic and glass. Then Brownie Wise appeared on the scene. Wise was a single mother, a hard-working, ambitious woman who brought Tupper great success with her concept for Tupperware parties. Women would fling open their homes and their social networks to sell plastic tubs galore at morning coffees and evening dinner parties.

Housewives transformed into businesswomen, the history of leftovers intersecting with the history of women's empowerment as the domestic universe of women received new recognition.

Brownie Wise also brought a touch of glamor to the Tupperware business. She would hurtle around in a pink Cadillac, dress in fancy haute couture, and put on a raucous party every year for the most successful "Tupper ladies." On one occasion, she arranged a sophisticated treasure hunt in a field. The ladies dug down into the soil and found goody bags filled with mink stoles, diamond rings, and tiny cars, their life-size equivalents standing in the parking lot ready to be driven away. At some point, the press hype surrounding Wise, not to mention her extravagance, became too much for Earl Tupper. He fired her and even scrubbed her name from the company's history—another story from the midcentury about women characterized by bullying, jealous men.

Nevertheless, the Tupperware parties remained, as did—unfortunately—the matter of leftover food, which would take on a new, global dimension in the decades that followed. Food waste became an international buzzword, referring not just to waste but to outright wastage. Today, human beings across the world throw away almost 20 percent of their food—food that is still edible. This is catastrophic for the climate, which is unnecessarily overburdened, and a smack in the face of the 830,000,000 people across the world who are experiencing starvation.

Let's take a quick look back through a couple of thousand years of human history. For eons, human beings would store their grain in clay pots buried in the earth and simply hope against hope that the harvest would yield enough to make it through the winter. Humans developed new trading routes at the cost of many lives, searching the world for foods that might be able to feed more mouths. Then came industrialization. Its achievements made it possible for human beings to stockpile food in previously unthinkable quantities and preserve it for decades. It heralded an age of abundant food—at least for most. What bitter irony it is that human beings theoretically solved the problem of hunger in the nineteenth century, and yet there are more people starving today than ever before.

Overproduction brings prices down, making food both more accessible and less valuable. The outright destruction and wastage of food eventually degenerated into the excess of recent times. People throw turnips away because they are crooked. They chuck packaged food in the garbage because they trust the best before dates more than their own noses, or because—the perennial dilemma of public kitchens with strict hygiene regulations—they don't know who has touched the packaging. They throw out food because the warehouses are too full.

Activists of a new stripe have arisen out of this excess: food waste heroes. Food has become a commodity that must be saved. These activists climb into supermarket dumpsters and retrieve edible food that has been thrown away. They push wholesalers to donate their excess stock to those in need, or simply travel around collecting wonky potatoes, odd tomatoes, and anything edible that is in oversupply. The hope—at least for the optimists among us—is that there is still time for this tale of recovering leftovers to become the story of how we saved good, edible food.

Hamburger
USA

The story of humanity is also a story of acceleration. Every human activity, every invention and piece of technology, is optimized from one generation to the next to operate with ever greater speed. In the age of industrialization, the pace ramped up ever more rapidly. In the early nineteenth century, there were still fears that a ride in a newfangled train could muddle a passenger's senses, that the mind was incapable of grasping where the body had traveled to at such a great speed. But trains only got faster, and then cars entered the scene and things really took off.

The manufacturing of these daredevil vehicles accelerated, too. Henry Ford was the first to have his cars manufactured on an assembly line, beginning in 1914. Before this, Frederick Winslow Taylor had revolutionized work in factories by optimizing workers' movements and stamping out anything deemed "unnecessary"—"eliminate all false movements, slow movements and useless movements"—until each employee became robotic, the most efficient of machines. Against this backdrop, it's no surprise that food, and the way it was manufactured and consumed, was subject to similar optimization fantasies. Fast food was the new maxim.

We're sticking in the USA for now—or, more precisely, the relatively uninteresting small town of San Bernardino, California. It was here where two brothers, Dick and Mac McDonald, ran a drive-in doing decent business, with pretty waitresses known as "carhops" serving hamburgers and a range of other popular snacks in the parking lot. Every day, the brothers would drive through the town's quiet streets in their shiny Cadillac and feel content. But after several years of comfortable boredom, they started craving a change. They wanted their business to be more lucrative, and faster, too. They came up with a radical idea that would have made Taylor proud, dubbing it the "Speedee Service System."

First, they fired the attractive waitresses, along with the cooks, all the other service staff, and even the dishwashers. Then they drastically cut back the menu. From now on, the only dishes they would serve wouldn't require cutlery or crockery. Instead, food was to be served in paper bags and drinks would come in paper cups. All that remained were hamburgers, cheeseburgers, and fries. Thousands of years of convention were swept away, and a large sign above the entrance declared civilization's brand-new credo: "Buy 'em by the bag!" The greatest changes were targeted at the kitchen, which now resembled a manufacturing hall. Cheap labor replaced trained cooks. These low-paid workers assembled the burgers using the same repetitive movements, like they were building small machines. Amid the rapid fire of orders, one worker grilled the patties, another placed the patty on the burger bun. Then—quick, quick!—another topped the patty with mustard, ketchup, onions, and pickles. The other half of the bun was placed on top aaaand . . . done. The hamburger cost just fifteen cents. The whole kitchen, with its different workstations, was adjusted with utmost precision to the employees' movements and the space required for those movements, so that burgers and fries could be served up with a kind of seamless choreography, a symphony of efficiency. The man at the counter taking orders stands with his back to the man at the burger preparation station; he is the only member of staff to come into contact with the public. This was the next radical act of efficiency: The customer must come up to the counter, order directly, and take their warm paper bag away with them.

When the McDonald brothers first transformed their drive-in, their customers could not fathom how it worked. They would stand in the parking lot, honking their car horns impatiently, not understanding why no one was coming out. However, this innovation was quickly accepted because it was quicker: Stressed-out office workers no longer had to spend their lunchbreaks making chitchat with waitresses on their inefficient routes between taking orders and bringing out food. Customers would now go in, order, and receive their food directly, enabling them to chow down with all the immediacy of an intravenous drip, without having to deal with the time-consuming fuss of cutlery. (On that note, it must be said that a burger tastes best when you hold it in your hands, each bite taking in the totality of the burger's architecture, that delicious combination of meat, bread, sauces, and spicy-sour toppings. Cut into its rapidly crumbling components using a knife and fork and the burger reveals itself to be a shapeless abomination made of inferior ingredients.)

Faster, higher, farther—these concepts drive humankind onward, and they are at the very heart of fast food. Efficient eating is also a product of the postwar era, an era of building and grappling, in which hard work leads to recognition. Eating quickly also means putting the individual and their cravings aside to rapidly feed workers performing hard graft. It's no surprise that, just a few decades later, when the concepts of individuality and attentiveness came back into focus in the food world, food preparation and consumption once again began taking a more leisurely pace and earned a new name: slow food.

Bánh Mì
Vietnam

Saigon in the 1950s. The wide boulevards are flooded
with bicycles and rickshaws, and a couple of cars honking their horns. Amid this swarm of traffic stands a lonely
policeman on a small pedestal, raising and lowering his
arms without gaining much attention from those around
him, like the conductor of some pompous orchestra. The
crowns of tall tamarind trees brush the façades of the
rows of houses, their delicate leaves quaking in the hot
air. Merchants drag their wares to the new Bến Thành
market. Conical straw hats tilt up and down. Elegant
ladies in tight silk dresses sit in street cafes under colorful awnings and observe the people walking by amid
the hustle and bustle. The French colonial era is coming
to an end, but everything is still permeated by a European spirit of savoir-vivre, which reveals itself in the numerous street stands piled with precarious displays of
long, golden baguettes. This is the home of the miracle

of Vietnamese French fusion cooking in sandwich form: the bánh mì.

Like any widespread street food, there are countless varieties of bánh mì (the term itself simply means "bread"), but the essence of this snack begins with a baguette. Here in Saigon, however, the baguettes are shorter than the original French bread that one might sport through the streets of Paris like a crunchy walking stick. Since the price of wheat is very high in Vietnam, the baguettes are made with rice flour, making their crusts even more crisp. The insides remain soft, pitted with holes where the moist, fragrant air has collected during baking. Up until the early 1950s, citizens of Saigon ate these modified baguettes every morning with butter and sugar, and street stalls offered them just the way the French knew and loved them: spread with butter, mayonnaise, or a little pâté and filled with ham.

The year 1954 saw Vietnam divided into two states and the French finally withdraw. Many Vietnamese people from the north of the country moved to the south; Saigon was churned up once more, leading to cultural explosions that could be felt in the very heart of Vietnam and beyond, to the country's culinary extremities, its street kitchens. It was at this historical moment that bánh mì revealed its previously unsuspected power. The baguette was still the foundation and shell of the bánh mì, and the pâté and mayonnaise also remained. But now the fillings went in a whole other, intensively flavorful direction thanks to chiles, fresh herbs like cilantro, raw vegetables, gherkins or pickled radish, grilled meat, and often a special variety of Vietnamese sausage flavored with fish sauce or a local version of headcheese. This hybrid sandwich of contrasting flavors would then be finished off with a couple of drops of Maggi sauce, which the French had brought with them from Switzerland. Bánh mì was culinary fusion at its finest, but more than anything, it was outrageously delicious.

If food is the essence of a culture, then the bánh mì is proof that this essence of a nation is constantly changing in appearance and taste. "Appropriation and adaptation are survival instincts for Vietnamese," writes Andrew Lam, "a land coveted by others and repeatedly colonized and dominated throughout the last thousand years."[33] China ruled over Vietnam for nearly a thousand years. This was followed by centuries of independence during which the country was reigned over by an ever-changing number of dynasties. And then came the French. Today, the debate still rages over whether another Vietnamese national dish, *phở bò* soup, has its etymological roots in the Cantonese phrase *luc pho*, meaning "beef with noodles," or whether it derives from the French *pot-au-feu*. On the subject of language more generally, Lam writes that Vietnamese is "an amalgamation of French, Chinese, local dialects of Khmer, Hmong, and Cham, and an array of other local tribal tongues."[34] This patchwork of identities is woven through all areas of life and is concentrated in the national cuisine.

Foreign food by definition means food that is unfamiliar. If this is true, then the French element had long since been devoured and appropriated by the time bánh mì became a cultural touchstone, as despite the fusion on display it was anything but foreign. Its identity had already been rewritten; the different influences fused together.

The baguette also has its own history. Baguettes were being baked in France as early as 1600 and were long considered the bread of the upper classes as they turned stodgy and stale so quickly that it was necessary to constantly buy fresh ones. But it was the impassioned Francophile travelers of the early twentieth century who took the image of the typical French baguette out into the world, and the Parisian boulangerie with its stacks of freshly baked baguettes became a place of longing imagination. And so, these long loaves were first declared a national symbol of France abroad before the French themselves adopted this outsider view, eventually embracing the baguette as part of their cultural heritage.

The colonial masters brought their feudal bread to a country where the colonized transformed it into something that could be sold cheaply from any street stand. This multi-layered amalgamation of national identities gave itself a good shake until it became something "typically Vietnamese," something that wore its blended nature clearly and with pride.

Then followed the Vietnam War, and bánh mì found its way to all four corners of the world, accompanying the Vietnamese refugees. Growing roots in the USA, it became integral to the flourishing food truck culture that emerged in the 1980s. Today, of course, you can continue to enjoy bánh mì on any street corner in Saigon or Ho Chi Minh City, while a tide of jostling mopeds rattles past in the background.

Toast Hawaii
West Germany

Like an eternally swinging pendulum, humanity's periods of deprivation and fear are followed by periods of ravenous overeating. Just think of the Middle Ages and the feasts that closely followed drought and spoiled harvests, or the feudal tables in Baroque princely houses overladen with roasted swans and towering sugar sculptures.

Postwar West Germany responded to the end of the darkest chapter in its history with abundance: buttercream cakes, thick emulsified sauces, mayonnaise, egg liqueur—and, of course, Toast Hawaii. A symbol of the cravings of the postwar period and a merciful dose of psychological repression were wrapped up in a square slice of bread and processed cheese.

"Good evening, gourmets!" declared Germany's first TV chef, stage name Clemens Wilmenrod, welcoming viewers to his show, *Bitte in zehn Minuten zu Tisch*, or "On the Table in Ten Minutes." His every movement on

TV was infused with an air of proud derision all his own. Wilmenrod was an actor by trade, albeit an unsuccessful one, and had a penchant for imaginative money-making schemes—covert advertising and product placement would eventually be his undoing. He is generally considered to be the inventor of Toast Hawaii (though it is highly probable that he was inspired by an advertisement from the American manufacturer of tinned ham).

What's sure is that in 1955 Wilmenrod publicly demonstrated how to make the dish. Take a slice of lightly toasted sandwich bread and spread it with a little butter. Top this with a slice of boiled ham and the crucial ingredient, from which the recipe takes its name, a slice of tinned pineapple, which has been sitting in sugary juice. Top this with a slice of processed cheese. (You can also top it off with a sticky sweet cocktail cherry for a cheeky touch of color.) Finally, place it in the oven for a few minutes. Watch out— the melted cheese and the hot pineapple can burn your mouth, as the pineapple releases its sweet, tangy juice into the cheesy topping. The white bread soaks everything up and rapidly loses its shape as it cools, transforming into a soggy mess that sates the desire for fat like a soothing, greasy comfort blanket. The combination of sweet and salty, which had long been absent from German cooking, seemed new and "exotic" to the palates of the 1950s. The two tastes collided, unchecked. Toast Hawaii is not a subtle dish. It doesn't offer a nuanced melding of flavors; it simply throws them together and hopes for the best.

Tinned pineapple was a much-coveted ingredient,

a bourgeois Aloha State fantasy. This exotic fruit contained a grand history of new worlds, of expeditions and the wanderlust of those who stayed behind. It was none other than Christopher Columbus who "discovered" pineapple for the Western world. On the island of Guadeloupe in 1493, he noticed that in front of each hut lay a bizarrely shaped fruit with prickly scales, topped with a bushel of thick leaves that stood up threateningly. As it turned out, these unusual objects served as a symbol of welcome. In the seventeenth century, the Dutch worked to cultivate the pineapple plant in their botanic gardens and their first greenhouses. In the eighteenth century, the British aristocracy followed suit and planted the fruit in their gardens. This proved a rather expensive affair, as the seedlings had to be planted in holes filled in with bricks, kept warm with mulch and horse manure, and covered with plate glass. In the winter, the plants would be moved into the greenhouses, which were heated by stoves.

Pineapples were considered an extra-special showpiece on dinner tables decorated with fruit. Those who could not afford to buy one would rent one from a fruit supplier for the evening. Their bizarre shape inspired porcelain manufacturers, goldsmiths, and architects. In the nineteenth century, greenhouses grew in size and the availability of pineapples grew alongside them. In 1829, the Paris exhibition *Carporama* presented stunned visitors with lifelike wax replicas of tropical plants and fruits that had previously been seen only in powdered or dried forms (such as coffee, cocoa, tea, and pepper), or that, like the pineapple, had only made an appearance in the homes of the elite. A whole world of fiery, sensuous colors and shapes exquisitely sculpted from wax seemed to be ready to burst from its showcases. Then, in the late nineteenth century, huge pineapple plantations were established (in Hawaii, of course) and tinned pineapple was introduced to the market. The fruit became a bulk commodity at last.

And now, Toast Hawaii saw the dream of palm beaches washing up into German kitchens. It was followed by Steak Hawaii; Schnitzel Hawaii; Fruit, Chicken, and Ham Salad Hawaii. Radio stations played a suitably fitting soundtrack: "Haiti Cherie," "Dreaming of the South Seas," and "The Rose of Tahiti," with ukuleles inevitably accompanying lyrics boasting a bracing lack of interest in authenticity. Hawaii remained a vague notion onto which anything could be projected, as in Vico Torriani's "Waikiki (Lips of Wine)": "Palm beaches / Skies so blue / Oh Waikiki / I can't forget you. / Kisses from Hawaii / So tender and nice / In Hawaii / You'll find true paradise."

The soothing sounds of Hawaiian music, the sweet luxuriance of so-called Hawaiian food—it all served to gently sedate a country that still lay in ruins. Trauma, as well as the question of the nation's guilt, was to be erased from the collective consciousness; attempts to rebuild and reappraise these would not follow until later. For the time being, Germany preferred to take a slice of American sandwich bread, oversweetened tropical fruit, greasy industrial cheese, and boiled ham, all of which had long been absent from their diets, and create a dish that promised modernity, cosmopolitanism, and perhaps even a shred of redemption in paradise. Just ten years after the end of the Nazi atrocities and an unimaginably brutal world war, Toast Hawaii became a minor meditation on the human capacity for forgetting.

The People's Noodle Soup
People's Republic of China

In the spring of 1958, every corner of China is shaken by a tremendous noise. Clanging and crashing echoes from roofs, alleyways, and fields. From four o'clock each morning, every Chinese citizen over the age of five is on their feet, taking to positions designated with precision by strategy headquarters, and begins with complete abandon to bash pots, plates, and anything that might make a noise, adding their shrill cries to the ruckus. China is defending its food—or, at least, that's what it thought.

Chairman Mao had declared that China would be visited by four plagues: mosquitoes, flies, rats, and sparrows. All four, he claimed, would bring disease and eat the people out of house and home. In Mao's view, the sparrows posed the greatest danger; though he would later be proven wrong, he was sure that the sparrows would devour the harvests in the fields and even eat the seeds in the barns. He called for the people to hunt sparrows, just one of the bizarre calls to action made during his campaign for the Great Leap Forward. The infernal racket made by the clanging pots and pans left the birds too scared to come down to rest and roost. It worked: For three days, little birds rained down from the sky, having died from exhaustion in the air. The winners in this unprecedented eradication effort were the locusts, whose numbers exploded now that they had no predators. Eventually, they stripped the fields bare.

A bad idea, perhaps? Certainly, and they kept coming. Mao wanted to reconfigure the whole country, imbuing the people with a socialist spirit, and so he imposed forced collectivization. Farmers were dispossessed, their kitchens emptied, their woks, pots, and dishes taken away, their hearths destroyed. From now on, comrades would be expected to eat in communal canteens. There, they could eat as much as they wanted—or such was the promise. The Communist Party's newspaper made a euphoric announcement: "In the not-too-distant future, the people's commune [. . .] will lead its members into a fairytale land, never before seen in history. An empire of freedom will bloom, and everyone will work according to his ability and receive as much as he needs."[35]

The ragtag bunch of farmers that made up the collectives would sit down together on a mismatched, colorful mix of chairs and stools stolen from farmhouses, astonished by the abundance of vegetables, rice dishes, noodle soups, steamed buns, thick porridge, and pork. (Pork was apparently Mao's favorite food, prepared for

him daily: red braised pork belly, slow-cooked in a mixture of soy sauce and Shaoxing rice wine, with ginger,
scallions, mint, star anise, and bay leaves.) No one really
understood where the lavish heaps of food on their plates
had come from—particularly as there was no one working
in the fields, as the farmers all had their hands full with
another mission.

In another bold measure, Mao had ordered furnaces to
be built across the country. These rickety constructions
were cobbled together by amateurs and could be found in
every backyard in China; the intention was for them to
run day and night. Chairman Mao hoped they would set
a powerful industrial revolution in motion. According to
his predictions, the optimism of which could hardly be
surpassed, China's steel industry would be stronger than
Britain's in fifteen years' time. Filled with confidence, the
Chinese threw everything they needed for daily life—including woks, pots, and agricultural machinery—into the
abyss of their makeshift furnaces. What emerged were
strange, molten lumps. The material was completely un-
usable: deformed, broken, useless scrap.

The first signs of the catastrophe to come were probably already noticeable in the communal kitchens. Where
once they had been able to eat as often as they liked and to
throw away leftovers without a worry, the people of China
soon found their food rationed. Subtle power struggles
played out in the simple act of serving soup. Some cooks
did not stir the pot of noodle soup properly and would
serve people little more than the thin broth from the top

of the pot. Only preferred diners would receive the soup underneath, filled with ingredients that had sunk to the bottom. As the people grew hungrier, gardens and fields had to be guarded overnight to protect against theft. Then there was little left besides corn rolls made with tree bark, watery grain porridge, and roots instead of noodles.

Not only that, but it was now impossible to bring the harvests in. The Great Leap Forward slid into a free fall heading for complete catastrophe; Mao's new orders for rural areas triggered the worst famine in human history. Since the nineteenth century, in large regions of the world, it was deemed that the state's highest duty was to provide citizens with food; the state was responsible for solving the problem of hunger. Mao's campaign constituted a dereliction of this duty. Once again, food was abused for political ends—it was barefaced propaganda and a means of deceiving the people who were filling their bellies in the communal canteens because nobody told them that in doing so, they were busy devouring the only available provisions. Of course, the chairman did not admit his mistake.

Even so, a few years later, the sparrows were no longer in the firing line. Though their complete eradication was unsuccessful, it did have unintended effects: With fewer around to keep insect populations in check, pest populations were booming. The new enemy of the people? Bedbugs.

Dehydrated Chicken Soup
Space

Human beings have always wanted to discover new frontiers. Human beings have also always needed to eat. The latter has frequently presented us with challenges. Tinned goods took us to the North Pole, but now, in the 1960s, human beings had set their sights on space. It was an undertaking that required a whole new kind of provisioning.

When the Russian cosmonaut Yuri Gagarin became the first man to journey into space, it was not entirely clear whether the human organism would even be able to consume food in zero gravity, or whether Gagarin would simply suffocate. Luckily for Gagarin, everything went according to plan, and he made it back down to Earth safe and sound. Nevertheless, you can imagine Gagarin looking at his dinner—two tubes, one of pureed meat and another of chocolate sauce—with somewhat mixed feelings. A little peeved at the Russians' success, the Americans soon announced that they would be the first nation to put a man on the moon.

An expedition to the moon in a twentieth-century rocket would take much less time than that journey to the North Pole a hundred years before, for which whole ships full of provisions had had to be taken along on the journey. The initial moon mission would require eight days' worth of provisions to feed the three astronauts involved: Neil Armstrong, Buzz Aldrin, and Michael Collins. However, space for provisions was limited, and even if it had been proven that human beings could eat in space, the absence of gravity presented those developing the astronauts' food with certain problems. In space, a sandwich posed a lethal threat: The crumbs, tiny particles of the crispy crust, could float around aimless and uncontrollable, and might, in a worst-case scenario, find their way into sensitive equipment or clog the filters inside the rocket's complex structure and paralyze it. Bread, one of the oldest and most significant foods in human history, had to be left behind on Earth. Dishes had to be prepared in such a way that no part of them would escape when they were opened or bitten into. The astronauts would be at risk of muscle wastage, so their food would need to supply them with protein, fats, vitamins, and carbohydrates—but they would need to manage without much fiber.

The first astronauts, like Gagarin, would squeeze easy-to-digest, nutrient-rich food into their mouths in the form of pastes from metal tubes. They also experimented with dishes pressed into bitesize cubes. Before the success of the first space flight, Russia fantasized about concentrating food into little pills—this was an old dream that had its origins in the late nineteenth century, a product of industrialization and the echoing memory of devastating famines. Although these super pills remained an impossible dream, even before the first moon landing, astronauts' food had progressed beyond tubes and cubes, mainly because this way of eating was deemed too unfamiliar and too technical. Human beings might be traveling to the moon, but they should remain human beings while they did so, complete with all their civilizational achievements: "You won't believe it, but we've got chicken soup up here!" cried astronaut Michael Collins over the radio, with all the puzzled euphoria of a traveler discovering their national dish is served at a tourist trap in the heart of a foreign city.

The solution was dehydration and freeze-drying. The Apollo 11 voyage took with it chicken soup, beef stew, spaghetti Bolognese, fruit loaf, and salad in the form of dry powder in plastic bags, which merely required the diner to add a little warm water. All you had to do next was knead the bag gently and—voilà!—you had dinner. There was also coffee in bags, black or with cream or sugar. The astronauts liked to drink it in quieter moments, while enjoying the view of Earth. Armstrong and Aldrin drank it to round off their first meal of the expedition (rehydrated bacon pieces, peaches, cookie cubes, and pineapple and grapefruit juice). Another high point regarding the power of food and drink to create ritual occurred when the capsule docked on the surface of the moon. Buzz Aldrin had smuggled along a wafer, as tiny as a fingernail, and a miniature bottle of wine: holy communion. He now pulled these out and embarked upon a "first supper" in space.

Astronaut food has only ever been consumed by a handful of people, yet it continues to shape the way we envision the food of the future. Its earliest forms—tubes, cubes, and powders—continually find their way into futuristic visions. In 1973, the film *Soylent Green* told the story of a distant future—2022, to be precise—in which the world's poor, at least, would subsist on synthetic red, yellow, and green tablets. In the film, a dystopian horror, the green tablet was revealed to be a concentrate of human flesh. In a more cheerful turn, in the 1997 film *The Fifth Element*, Milla Jovovich, alias Leeloo Minai Lekatariba-Lamina-Tchai Ekbat, places a super pill in the oven, opening it seconds later to pull out an enormous, sizzling roast chicken complete with vegetable trimmings. In *The Force Awakens* (2015), somewhere in the grim world of the *Star Wars* universe, scavenger Rey has had a stressful day, but when she tips powder into some hot water, the mixture immediately grows into a loaf of bread—a soothingly homey morsel.

Space travelers are alienated from Earth, which suddenly appears immeasurably far away. They are also alienated from their own bodies; floating in zero gravity leads their muscles to waste away and their faces to swell. They lose their sense of taste as the lack of gravity apparently leaves them with constantly blocked noses. And so even chicken soup, though it seems familiar at first, tastes strange and bland, having already been deconstructed by the dehydration process. To combat the blandness, they season their food with a little salt water, pepper mixed with oil (like bread crumbs, loose grains of salt and pepper are on no account allowed to go floating around the inside of the rocket) or a particular favorite: hot sauce. And so, soup in a plastic bag takes on a greater significance, permitting this little foreign body, traveling through space, to experience a taste of home. Even the future has its moments of nostalgia.

Buffet

West Germany

In the early 1970s, the German singer-songwriter Rein-hard Mey sang, "At a hot fight at the cold buffet / A man could still be a man / An eye for an eye, aspic and jelly / We'd see who could really take a stand. [. . .] A woman dreams, smiling, of a hero's death / Swimming in caviar and Champagne / All the while she's stuffing the leftovers in her bag / It's a lightning-quick robbery campaign."

The *Wirtschaftswunder*, the West German "economic miracle," saw many middle-class households in the Federal Republic of Germany enjoying a period of stability and moderate wealth. After several dark decades for politics and humankind alike, people were happy to celebrate again. Family parties, anniversaries, birthdays—they all offered a welcome excuse to invite a gaggle of guests over. However, there was no longer the space, let alone the staff—the maid profession was gradually dying out—for the kind of seated dinner once idealized by previous generations, with a seating plan, hot food, and ironed damask napkins. Instead, there was a new trend, a kind of meal that had existed before, but that now perfectly suited the circumstances and the spirit of the age: the buffet. "At many parties, a cold buffet is not only pleasant for the guests, but also practical for the hostess," declares *Kalte Küche von A–Z*, or *A–Z of Cold Cuisine*, published in 1977. "It also makes it possible to cater for a large number of guests in small spaces."

It's Saturday afternoon and the doorbell to Auntie Gudrun and Uncle Günther's house won't stop ringing; it's their silver wedding anniversary. Their modern, postwar apartment has been spruced up: A shelving unit with built-in minibar spans the wall and has been polished to a high sheen, and the first LP of the afternoon is playing on the record player. That morning, there was considerable fanfare as Uncle Günther pushed the dinner table against the wall, just as the A-to-Z guide recommends: "Place the biggest table in your home next to the wall or in the middle of the room, ensuring that the path to the buffet, around the buffet, and from the buffet to the seating area is as clear as possible."[36]

This informal way of presenting food would have been largely unfamiliar to Uncle Günther's parents. In Louis Fritzsche's *Illustrierte Tafelkultur*, or *Illustrated Table Culture*, from 1918, the buffet is addressed, but it is perceived as something of a stopgap, intended for situations where a well-set table is not possible—for instance, when arranging a private concert at home, to which "so many invitations are extended that the space does not permit one to seat guests around tables." In this case, a buffet was a must, and the issue of space was to be concealed with pompous decoration, ideally several vases of flowers. Fritzsche also recommends erecting an Oriental tent over the buffet, adding, "service for a buffet of this kind [. . .] requires around six staff."[37]

However, Auntie Gudrun's followed the more modern A-to-Z's advice and spread several layers of plastic wrap over the table—she found it going for cheap in a specialty store. She prepared most of the dishes the day before; they will all be eaten cold anyway. (This is another simplifying step—no need to fuss over different temperatures, no smells emanating from the hot oven.) And of course, there will be no one standing at the buffet, on call to serve the guests. Everyone will serve themselves, hence the need to clear a path around the table, to avoid the scenes of carnage described in Mey's song and to ensure that everyone can pile food onto their plates and make it back to their seats safely. Guests find somewhere to sit and return to their conversations or make small talk. The traditional patter of dinner table conversation comes to an abrupt end with the move to buffets, as someone is always getting up to fetch themselves a second helping, interrupting any rigorous conversation and leading to a relaxed culture of chitchatting.

The buffet marks a liberation from the stiff dinner table talk that had developed over previous centuries. It's the end of ascending in an orderly manner to the dinner table at the prompt, "Dinner is served," with the man of the house seated at the top of the table, deciding when dinner begins and ends. It is the end of countless sets of cutlery with various functions. No one serves the dishes or takes them away. There is something light and playful about this democratization of food. While fast food reflects a radical simplification in dining habits, the buffet radiates a flamboyant, festive joy that is also expressed in the ever-greater number of colorful skewers used to decorate all the appetizers. Buffet classics such as the meat (or cheese) hedgehog, toadstool-like tomato-topped eggs, deviled eggs, and pumpernickel skewers emerged as a result of this almost childlike tendency toward playing with our food.

Auntie Gudrun has arranged the buffet dishes, complete with colorful little flags, like artifacts pinned in a museum display case. A dinner eaten in several courses resembles an opera performed in consecutive acts, but at the buffet, the starter, main, and dessert all charge ahead at once in a jumble of dishes. Even so, they follow a certain order from left to right: There is a cold beetroot soup, turkey breast with three kinds of cranberry sauce, three different rice salads (one with smoked fish, one with tomatoes, and one with curry and chicken), meatloaf from a tin, two cheese dishes (a Camembert spread and a cream of Roquefort). Fresh pineapple adds a touch of the exotic, just as in the days of the Victorians, who would rent them to use as centerpieces. On the far right, a cream cake with cherries sits proudly before a large punch bowl, which tops off the spread. Most guests follow the order in which the dishes are arranged. But depending on when you got up to go to the buffet, one person will already be standing in front of the dessert, while another is busy serving themselves some cold soup—another deviation from the convention that assumes each course will be eaten by all the diners at the same time. Freedom to choose, for guests and hosts alike.

There is only one convention, one ritual, to which a buffet adheres, and it is still upheld to this day: None of the dishes can be touched until a certain number of guests have gathered. The dishes wait, frozen in their comical get-up. Once the host decides that the time is right, they utter those four special words that bring a sense of relief, pulling an invisible curtain to one side: "The buffet is open!"

The Gatsby Sandwich
South Africa

It begins with a stick of white bread sliced down the middle, as thick and as long as an arm. Then come the fillings: *polony*, a sausage similar to mortadella, a big heap of fries, and a hearty portion of fried eggs and salad. These salty and fresh flavors are joined by something on the spicier side, such as Indian achar (fruits and vegetables pickled in vinegar, oil, chile, and spices) or peri-peri sauce, which mainly comprises hot chile peppers and garlic. To get a bite of this multilayered monster, you have to get a strong grip on it and press down so that an infusion of spicy-tangy fat and protein all but shoots into your mouth, a well-aimed punch of the interculturality that defines South Africa's culinary spectrum. There will be many variations on the Gatsby sandwich in the years to come, but they will all have two things in common: Once this beast of a sandwich is ready, it is wrapped up to take away—it is never eaten in. And it is always cut into four.

The Gatsby is inextricably linked to Athlone, a suburb of Cape Town. In the 1950s, this area was just sand, thick undergrowth, and a few farmhouses accompanied by small, dry vegetable fields, antelopes roving among them. As part of the Group Areas Act, these inhospitable patches of earth became densely populated, predominantly with people of color who were forced out of the central city districts and forcibly resettled here under Apartheid. Apartment complexes, small houses, and huts sprawled across the dusty land. Since the new inhabitants of Athlone had to go to the great trouble of commuting into the city to their poorly paid jobs, they no longer had much time to cook. As a result, fast food joints began popping up across the neighborhood, providing cheap food to take away. In South Africa, take-out culture has a political slant because Black people were generally not allowed to eat in restaurants until well into the 1990s.

The Gatsby was invented in 1976, the year the uprising in Soweto was brutally crushed, prompting nationwide unrest among the country's Black population. The story goes that Rashaad Pandy, owner of a fish and chip shop in Athlone, had promised four men a free meal in return for help renovating his shop. Unfortunately, there was practically no food left, so, in a flash of culinary inspiration, Pandy came up with an enormous sandwich made from leftovers: sausage, fries, salad, fried eggs, and achar. The original Gatsby was made with a round loaf of Portuguese bread, which he cut into four pieces. One of the workers bit into the sandwich and happily declared it "a Gatsby smash"—an allusion to the lavish opulence of *The Great Gatsby*. (The Robert Redford film had recently been showing in cinemas.)

The next morning, Pandy began selling his new creation in the shop under the name "the Gatsby." Several customers said they struggled to hold the round bread, so Pandy began using longer stick-shaped loaves. Regardless of whether the sandwich originated quite as the story suggests, this is what has been told ever since. It is part of the Gatsby's identity, a story of collaboration. One person invents the dish as a gesture of thanks, another inspires the name, and other people help improve its shape. The Gatsby is a joint effort through and through, all the way to diners' bellies. Due to its size, the Gatsby is always shared between four, just like the first time. When it is ready, it is taken away to be enjoyed by a group, because at the time of its invention it couldn't be eaten inside. The Gatsby stands for exclusion and community all at once.

In the years that followed, the Gatsby remained a product of community that everyone could enrich with their own ideas. In an era of oppression, here was something that everyone was free to participate in shaping. A new filling was added: steak seasoned with masala spices. There are other versions that include chicken and cheese, whole sausages, and goulash. Pandy also started offering a version containing fried fish or calamari alongside the original. All these versions were united by a fearlessness when it came to using numerous fat-laden ingredients (fries were a staple) from a wide range of culinary cultures, as well as the sheer size of the dish, which could not be conquered solo.

In the 1980s, Athlone developed into a center of resistance against the ruling white regime. The local fast-food restaurants would stay open until late in the evening on days when rallies were held so that activists could eat out afterward. It is easy to imagine numerous Gatsbys being passed over the counter, their portions distributed among the gesticulating hands of demonstrators as they continued to debate and plan. Even in ancient Rome, the ruling class tried time and again to shut down the plebeian taverns for fear of conspiracy. In South Africa's ghettos and townships, instead of plebeian taverns there were fast food shops, spaces in which to communicate over a sandwich—a sandwich made to share. Food builds community—and nurtures community resistance.

Several years after Apartheid ended, the Gatsby suddenly appeared in public discourse once more. A white food stylist and cook, born in Cape Town, posted a video of her own version of the sandwich, with chopped spinach, curry, mayonnaise, potato wedges, plum chutney, and arugula, wrapped in the snug, Eurocentric embrace of a ciabatta. The residents of Cape Town's suburbs were up in arms over this act of appropriation. The Gatsby stood for the section of society that ultimately rebelled; it stood for local pride in the area where it was first invented. If you travel to Athlone today, you'll be quick to spot a huge mural bearing the words, "Home of the Gatsby."

Liquid Olives
Spain

It's almost the new millennium. Across the world, people fear technological collapse will hit the night the ball drops. The new year ultimately arrives without event, but is swiftly followed by the shock of 9/11, a fundamental turning point for many. The radio plays the same depressing song by Enya twenty-four hours a day and people stand and stare, frightened and dumbfounded by the horrors of which human beings are capable.

At some point during these years, permeated with a gloomy sense of the End Times, gourmet food critics began raving about a completely new kind of food, a clever new way of playing with expectations and old patterns of perception. Dishes you expected to be sweet were bitter, foods you thought would be firm would melt, dishes traditionally served hot and steaming would be flash frozen. Cutting-edge cuisine was all about foams, spheres, and textures. Plates would be mired in dramatic artificial mist. An unsuspecting diner would take a spoonful of their seemingly normal pea soup and realize that it had been cleverly deconstructed: One pea would dissolve into frothy air, while another pea would turn out to be ice cream, and the next would burst between the diner's teeth.

At the center of this avant-garde cooking, known as "molecular gastronomy," was El Bulli, a restaurant on the edge of a scenic bay in the Costa Brava. Initially a beach bar, it grew to become a three-Michelin-star restaurant under the creative leadership of Ferran Adrià. In the mid-nineties, Adrià adapted the former head chef's kitchen and embarked on his first experiments. Awestruck whispers claimed that El Bulli activated a phone line for a single day in January to take reservations. In half an hour, all the tables for the following year would be booked. The select few who witnessed this Catalonian spectacle talked of foamed smoke, melon juice caviar, melting croquettes, carrot air, a balloon made of paper-thin Gorgonzola, and delicate leaves of dehydrated mango puree. The thirty courses of deconstructed dishes were served—subverting expectations—amid stunningly old-fashioned interiors. The dining room looked like something out of an outdated hacienda, with ornamental floor tiles, dark, heavy wooden chairs, red velvet cushions, and creaking roof beams. This dusty time capsule was where the future of food was taking off.

Here's an iconic dish from Adrià's culinary laboratory: spherified olives. Olives would be pitted and pureed, then pressed through a cloth to extract their juice. The juice would then be mixed with thickening agents and dropped into a bath of cold water and alginate powder using a small measuring spoon. The calcium chloride in the olives immediately separated from the alginate and formed a firm skin around the liquid: It was simple chemistry. The new, bodiless olives were taken out of the water bath and placed in a jar filled, very traditionally, with olive oil, rosemary, and lemon pieces. They would be served to diners the next day, suitably camouflaged as plain old preserved olives. The waiter would fish out an olive and pass it on a spoon to the diner, who would be puzzled at first. Then the surprise would come, the subversion of what was expected. The false olive exploded in the diner's mouth, prompting an expression of frenetic delight. It was pure flavor—the intense, salty essence of the olive—or, as *New York Times* columnist Mark Bittman put it, stunned and without a hint of irony: "An olive made of an olive. This is art imitating life."

Food as avant-garde art: It was not for nothing that Ferran Adrià was the first chef to be invited to present his dishes at the art exhibition Documenta 12 in 2007. And when, shortly before the exhibition opened, he somewhat eccentrically canceled his appearance at Kassel, saying it would be impossible for him to achieve there what he was capable of creating at El Bulli, it did nothing to detract from the international admiration for his creations. For another four years, until the restaurant ultimately closed in 2011, his fans did everything in their power to be able to take a seat on one of his restaurant's fifty uncomfortable chairs and taste the food that imitated life itself.

Molecular chefs argue that they are capturing the essence of a food, that by transforming a dish into an aromatic foam, they are paying homage to it and elevating it to the level of an idea. Food becomes an intellectual experience. But more than anything, this kind of petri dish cooking marks a profound moment of estrangement between human beings and the food they eat.

It is no coincidence that molecular gastronomy witnessed its heyday at a time when human beings were carelessly and fatalistically destroying the environment around them at a greater rate than ever before. They had completely lost their connection to nature. Pipette in hand, they laughed in the face of Creation; these olives might have been growing on trees for thousands of years, but we can create olives that explode in your mouth—so ha! Gimmickry and imitation techniques had long been commonplace on dining tables—just look at the culinary art of antiquity. What was new was the transformation of food into something weightless and lacking in substance. With his foams and dry fog, Adrià was hollowing food out, disembodying it until it floated above the plate like a mirage.

Had the people of the new millennium arrived in the future?

Naked Roast Lamb
United Kingdom

"It's gotta be simple. It's gotta be tasty. It's gotta be fun."
These were the words with which the English chef Jamie
Oliver, then just twenty-four years old, introduced viewers to his new cookery show. *The Naked Chef* first arrived
on the UK's screens on the BBC in 1999. Oliver probably
had no idea what he was about to unleash. The age-old
cultural practice of cooking had made the transition to
media event decades before, and in the meantime it had
become a key feature of everyday programming. Even so,
until this point cookery programs had been somewhat di-
dactic in their aspirations. Chefs would speak directly to
the camera, explaining a recipe to their audience, which
initially comprised housewives and later included any
adult with access to a kitchen. By contrast, in these early
years, Jamie Oliver never spoke to the camera. He broadcast from a pointedly *normal* kitchen that was clearly
part of a comically small London flat. While he cooked,

he would spend the whole time chatting to a person off camera, dispelling any notion of the TV chef as lecturer.

Oliver celebrated a genuine, wild joy of cooking that drew a whole generation of twentysomethings into the kitchen. He was also deliberately untechnical; his cooking was free of pretentious ingredients and techniques—naked, even, as his show's title suggested. He would smash cloves of garlic with a wine bottle, squeeze lemons using just his hands, flail the cheese grater about, smear butter with his fingers, crush coriander seeds in a rustic stone mortar, all while grinning wildly. In the very first episode, he nonchalantly speared holes in a joint of lamb without any special professional tricks before stuffing the holes with garlic and herbs. Oliver's show focused on the lovely little moments that cooking entails: potatoes turning crispy in hot butter in the oven; the sizzling skin of a roast chicken; warm melting chocolate wrapped in pastry; a fragrant lamb roast carved into thick slices on a rough wooden board. This was interspersed with footage of Oliver heading to the market on his little Vespa and buying vibrant chiles, chatting with other cooks, returning home to the pot simmering on the stove and soon opening the door to a friend who happened to be passing by. *The Naked Chef* not only demonstrated how to cook delicious food, it also offered up a whole way of life, a life that was urban, convivial, hip, and full of pleasure. Cooking became a lifestyle.

It had far-reaching consequences too, because social media was taking off at the same time as Oliver, who shot to fame and whose influence suddenly saw students hosting dinner parties in their flat shares. And since food, one of humanity's essential needs, was suddenly cool, it was now being distributed and presented in entirely new ways. This included taking photographs of food. Smartphones came into existence and were soon followed by apps and filters that enabled diners to present their food in particularly aesthetic ways. Eating became a visual experience, spreading across the internet at speed. A significant term first appeared online in 2004: "food porn." Today, innumerable images of food can be found under this hashtag. The term refers to dishes that are almost obscenely appetizing in appearance, and that are observed with a certain voyeuristic longing: pizza dripping with cheese and grease, huge burgers slick with sauce, opulent cakes, steaks on platters—all the targets of hungry, lustful eyes. There is a clear proximity to the "feast for the eyes" of the Baroque still life, but there is one fundamental difference: These seventeenth-century paintings typically portray raw, unprepared food. Fruit, vegetables, and crustaceans are perishable, but they are arranged in their fresh, unadulterated state. By contrast, food porn images reveal a moment of even greater ephemerality, a glimpse of a dish ready to eat. They are more vivid, steaming and spilling out of their bounds—captured in a quick photo and then gobbled right up. These photos are less a feast for the eyes than a tease for the belly and the mouth, which will already be watering.

This phenomenon sees food become a commodity to be consumed on a number of levels—directly, but also digitally as a source of aesthetic pleasure and a catalyst for desire. Food also becomes an expression or sign of a community and a lifestyle—and this brings us back to Jamie Oliver. His career began at the turn of the millennium and the period of general unease that followed 9/11, during which many people withdrew into domesticity and their immediate, safe family lives. Oliver was cooking for these people, offering them an emotional safe space. His comfort food is ultimately food porn: dishes rich in carbohydrates and fat that you can "just dig into." But they are also dishes that give us an immediate sense of well-being and awaken a certain nostalgia. Pasta, pizza, stews—it all tastes like childhood, like something cooked from the heart. While the avant-garde cooking that was flourishing at the same time was creating food with the greatest technical effort, disembodying and uncoupling it from anything natural, Oliver was kneading his bread by hand and crushing garlic cloves for a hearty roast, letting us happily take a seat at his kitchen table while the cold world outside faded away to the sound of cooking pots gurgling contentedly.

Mushroom and Mussel Broth on Hay
Kingdom of Denmark

Imagine a small bundle of hay, arranged with precision in a simple bowl. Nearby sits a small jug of steaming broth, unclouded and black-brown in color, silky fat glistening on its surface. This is poured over the hay. In seconds, the hay absorbs as much broth as it can. Then, wild and irrepressible, like an exploding mophead, the bundle bursts open, filling the bowl like a flower in bloom. The diner places the bowl to their lips and slurps the broth through the hay, which exudes the scent of a sun-warmed summer meadow. The broth tastes earthy and salty, like the forest and the sea. The little spectacle that sees the hay burst open is no molecular magic trick—it is sheer nature.

Since the turn of the millennium, the collective consciousness has woken up, much like the blooming bundle of hay—though much slower, in tortuous, snail-like slow motion (and the process is still ongoing)—to the idea that it cannot go on like this. The brief age of humankind is already threatening to collapse. It was this somnambulistic realization that saw a restaurant open in Copenhagen, a restaurant that prompted a worldwide culinary movement. The restaurant, of course, was Noma, under the creative leadership of a highly driven individual, head chef René Redzepi. It was his idea to cook with ingredients found in the restaurant's immediate vicinity. This aspiration toward regionality was especially radical in a country where practically nothing grows for many months of the year. Even more surprising—and often, at first glance, seemingly inedible—were the products that he found and introduced to the table (and here was the radical aspect; nouvelle cuisine was also inspired by regional cooking): fermented moss, caramelized honeybee larvae, pears preserved with salt from wood ants. The repertoire is often very simple: a little egg yolk, a humble potato, and a couple of elderflower blossoms; a flatbread with rose petals; sheep's milk mousse with a granita of meadow grasses; leeks with ash, hazelnut, yogurt, and caramelized chicken sauce.

At first, Redzepi's concept stood for a new Nordic cuisine—new because it was more extreme and uncompromising than everything that had previously been fermented, preserved, and cooked in Scandinavia. Redzepi was also one of the key figures in the "Nordic Kitchen Manifesto" in 2004, which promoted embracing regional and traditional foods and returning to manual food production. It expressed a longing that had seized people across the world post-millennium: a longing for what was handmade, for small, local manufacturers and generations-old family businesses. This vision of a socially acceptable, aesthetic sustainability spread to numerous areas of life, such as furniture design, fashion, printing, travel, and especially the culinary arts, all the way to alcoholic spirits, which were now being produced in the smallest of distilleries, ideally with labels printed on some obscure, old-fashioned machine.

Previously, molecular gastronomy had deconstructed food and hollowed it out with the aim of outdoing nature, but Redzepi's cooking took the opposite position. It elevated the produce, glorifying leeks, worshipping meadow grasses. Humankind had almost completely conquered and destroyed nature, and now it was trying to have a relationship with it. (Interestingly, around the time that Noma and Redzepi were rapidly gaining recognition, one of the restaurants at the forefront of molecular gastronomy, El Bulli, closed.) Not long ago, humanity had placed itself at the apex of Creation, and now it was groveling before it, sniffing blissfully at hay. Redzepi achieved all this by preparing a limited number of ingredients perfectly and by hand, with the constant aim of showcasing the produce in all its aromatic beauty. He combined his culinary techniques with the idea of the uncompromising restaurant, of foraging in the local environment. (It was this more than anything that made his restaurant famous, and it would soon receive a surfeit of stars and awards; a unique literary genre soon emerged that could well be called "foraging with Redzepi"—writers and journalists would travel to the far North to walk through forests and meadows with the calm and friendly chef and try everything that was growing.) This idea saw humanity returning to its ancestors, to the hunter-gatherers who walked in nature and took and ate whatever they could find.

The return to the hunter-gather connection with nature made great waves in high-end gastronomy (though pinecones, moss, and ants cost nothing, processing them for Michelin-star cuisine is so expensive that not everyone could afford to enjoy the new deification of nature), and many restaurants followed suit with a similar approach. There was talk of "brutal locality" or "alchemical nature cuisine" that saw chefs cooking with stone pigments or even placing pumpkins on top of ant hills, so that the fruit could be broken down by the ants' formic acid before being vacuumed up and turned into a puree.

Even though this was a somewhat elitist style of cooking, the crucial and fundamental view was that no one should be importing exotic products from the other side of the world in order to create sophisticated dishes. Unfortunately, many a well-meaning but rather less innovative chef would overstep the mark and dogmatically serve up whole charred leeks, or a slice of some mediocre fish from a nearby pond, albeit one killed using a cool, ancient technique. In moments like these, you find yourself hoping that not every ingredient on an overpriced ten-course menu has been foraged from the abandoned parking lot behind the restaurant. Burned brambles remain just that. And the hunter-gatherers of the last Ice Age would have thought so, too.

Nomura Jellyfish Salad

Japan

It's the late aughts and we're somewhere off the coast of Japan, near Tokyo. It's a cool morning and a fishing boat glides gently through the water. A lone fisherman leans on the boat's rail and looks out at the sea. Suddenly, he jumps and cries out. In the depths beneath and surrounding the entire boat as far as the horizon, the water is full of enormous jellyfish. They float in the direction of the land, like aliens in an apocalyptic sci-fi fantasy, mute and unrelenting. Their huge bodies, up to two meters wide, are like gleaming bells, like mushroom caps dragging meter-long tentacles behind them. These are Nomura jellyfish, and in recent years they have regularly haunted the waters off Japan, like a plague of Biblical proportions. These mighty creatures approach, somehow, from the seas around China or South Korea (nobody wants to investigate this question too closely) and they are a product of global warming and overfishing. They make fishing nets stick, squash or cover the other fish in slime, and have even been known to capsize ships. In short, they present an out-of-control catastrophe fresh from the depths of the ocean, where a complex balance has gone haywire.

A similarly uncanny situation had emerged a few years earlier in the US, in the rivers of the state of Washington. An anxious citizen had bought two snakehead fish—a delicacy native to China—intending to make soup for his sister who was unwell. As the sister was convalescing by the time the fish were delivered, the creatures were kept in a home aquarium where they quickly grew. Snakeheads are strikingly ugly fish with sharp, predatory teeth. When they grew too big for their tank, the man put the fish in a pond behind a shopping mall. Unfortunately, snakeheads can survive for several days on land, where they can cover considerable distances by positioning their fins vertically and using them to crawl over the earth. What began as two fish in a fish tank culminated in the breed spreading to the Potomac River and its tributaries, where they began munching their way through everything these waters had to offer thanks to their sizable appetites.

A few years later, crayfish with lurid black and red shells scuttled through the rainy streets of the Berlin embassy district, strolling in their droves along footpaths in *Tiergarten*, bathing in waterways and lakes in the parks, and happily spreading the crayfish plague. They were Louisiana crawfish, to be precise, and had probably been released by animal-loving aquarium enthusiasts. Now, their overpopulation was destroying whole waterways.

Since humans have been touring and exploiting the Earth on a grand scale, they have also had to deal with invasive species. What can be done to combat these domineering plants and animals? The most promising method of protecting different ecosystems from complete invasion by aggressive invaders entails setting another, larger aggressor after them. Ideally the most dangerous predator on the planet: humankind. Human beings simply have to eat these invasive creatures before they strip everything bare.

No other species on Earth has been able to adapt so effortlessly to sources of food running low. No more mammoths? No problem, we'll just eat buffaloes! In theory, human beings will eat anything, and they are the only creature capable of making anything palatable—for the most part—through cooking, stewing, marinating, fermenting—you name it. The phenomenon of invasive species sees the pendulum swinging in a new direction: Suddenly, there is an oversupply of a particular product. Not only that, but it is threatening every other kind of food, so people must sit down to dinner immediately before there is nothing left but wall-to-wall jellyfish. After all, these animals could be the food of the future. Unlike many other creatures, these are thriving in the dystopian conditions that climate scientists have been warning of for decades, so we are unlikely to run out of them any time soon. Scientists are already talking about "the rise of slime." And perhaps that works in our favor; our species is so successful when it comes to surviving and multiplying that, gradually, an inevitable question arises: What else are we supposed to eat? The jellyfish could save us one day. Not only is it apparently impossible to decimate their species, but they are also very healthy—their amorphous bodies are free from fat and cholesterol, but rich in protein, sodium, calcium, potassium, and magnesium.

In China, where Nomura jellyfish is a popular delicacy, people have long been aware of its benefits. They are preserved and dried in salt so the jellyfish becomes crisp (when air-dried, they turn to dust; when cooked, there is little left but sticky slime). Another recipe sees dried jellyfish prepared with garlic, soy sauce, and cilantro, after having been rehydrated in water. They become glassy strips, a little slippery but firm, like rice noodles that are not quite cooked. Jellyfish are also eaten in Japan, where they are enjoyed in spiced marinades, in salads, and in soups. A European research team by the name of *Go Jelly* set itself a goal of making jellyfish socially accepted in Western cuisine. With a global population nearing nine billion people, venison and pâté-loving Europeans will eventually be unable to avoid getting up close and personal with these slippery creatures. And so, scientists have worked out a few suggested dishes: jellyfish carpaccio, Mediterranean jellyfish soup, jellyfish sous-vide with faux caviar, and jellyfish with noodles and sesame sauce.

The idea of not just eating invasive animals and plants but turning them into hip delicacies is becoming the model for the future. Berlin's Louisiana crawfish can be found as crayfish and brioche sandwiches and as the base for bouillabaisse. The Chinese mitten crab, another invasive species, is a reasonable lobster substitute. In the USA, where the Asian shore crab and rampant butterbur have spread nationwide, a restaurant has opted to use them as ingredients for sushi.

It is human beings who prompted these invasions of species, big and small, on land and in the water, so it is only right that they pick up the tab—and it could well be a tasty one. We should proceed with caution, however: Fail to properly remove the poisonous tentacles of the Nomura jellyfish before eating and they pose a serious danger to the diner. Yet another thorn in the side of humanity worldwide.

Pandemic Dinner
Worldwide

In early 2020, a pandemic broke out and transformed cities, towns, and villages worldwide into something out of an apocalyptic science fiction movie. People barricaded themselves in their homes, and in some parts of the world, the military patrolled the empty streets. Faces disappeared behind face masks. The inhabitants of the Earth distanced themselves from one another. Unable to shake a constant feeling of dreamlike absurdity, lonely shoppers—wrapped up to keep out the germs—drifted past glass refrigerated counters at the supermarket filled with plastic-wrapped goods and studied the information on boxes of rationed products. These months—or years—of social distancing did something to us. They prompted society-wide debates about how we really want to live our lives. Much of this discourse centered on food: isolation and community, panic buying and fear, solace, longing, healing, and the dream of self-sufficiency.

Sharing a meal together is a cornerstone of human existence. During the lockdowns, this became clearer than it had been for a long time. During the pandemic, many families, trapped together at home, went back to gathering around the dinner table. The classic three meals a day, previously dismissed as outdated and inflexible, now gave a sense of structure to daily lives that had become a never-ending stream of working from home and home-learning. In contrast, restaurants were off limits and dinner parties were banned. So, people ate together on video calls, organizing digital multi-course menus and wine tastings. The shared table that bears the dishes that we all smell, taste, and enjoy together in unison became a virtual phenomenon, as did the flood of images of our culinary creations that poured into cyberspace with renewed force. This time, it was less about food porn than about taking pride in homemade food. During the pandemic, people were cooking and baking like there was no tomorrow. Grocers recorded explosive rises in sales of spicy sauces and exotic vegetables. More flavor, more of the unknown, was finding its way into home cooking; wanderlust simmered in steam cookers and newly purchased woks. And people were baking again—bread, inordinate quantities of bread, as their ancestors once had. That was, until they stared at the emptiness of the supermarket shelves aghast. For the first time in several generations, people experienced what it was like when the flour runs out.

Those who didn't cook were having food delivered. Contact-free deliveries were the perfect solution. Simply open the door in your mask to pick your delivery off the doormat, where a similarly masked delivery person would deposit it like a ticking bomb before retiring to the safety of the stairwell. The food lay isolated in its impermeable boxes and bags.

Pizza was the most common order worldwide. The number one greasy, doughy comfort food, the melting cheese like a warm hug. It was soothing, like all the sweet-smelling baked goods in our ovens that lulled our senses, like the sweet candy that provided a moment of distraction, or all the small, delicious snacks that were now selling like hot cakes. The comfort food backlash has been a reliable companion to every global crisis in recent decades, with clear parallels to the Middle Ages, when every famine was followed by feasting and bingeing. The Middle Ages also reared its head in a newly rekindled interest in the healing powers of certain dishes. Dietary supplements, thought to strengthen the body's defenses in the face of the circulating virus, were suddenly on sale everywhere, as were fruits and vegetables, preferably from local, organic farms. People wanted their bodies to be as vigorous and resilient as nature itself. Now, everyone was fantasizing about becoming self-sufficient. Baking bread, canning foods, preserving, and fermenting—it just wasn't enough. In World War I, no patch of land was deemed too small for growing potatoes. And now, salads, herbs, and vegetables were being grown on window ledges, balconies, and urban waste ground in addition to gardens. A community garden became every hipster's ultimate dream. Waiting lists for community garden plots grew exponentially. We were retreating ever further into our little cocoons.

And then, just like that, the nightmare was over. We wrenched open the doors of our now carefully decorated apartments and sprinted back into restaurants and into the arms of the loved ones we had gone so long without embracing. Breadmaking machines and Santoku knives gathered dust on our shelves.

What will remain of this exceptional time in which we ate pandemic dinners and cooked to excess? Futurologists believe that people will take a greater interest in food that can be "experienced." "For consumers, this begins with shopping at a weekly market, from farms, bakers, butchers, or delicatessens, where they can talk, smell, taste or get a sense of the atmosphere of the site where their food was produced," argued the 2021 Food Report from the Future Institute.

Food as an experience for all the senses? It would be a wonderful thing. The more we learn about our food, the more consciously we enjoy its flavors and its abundance, the more we can—hopefully—take responsibility for our edible resources. If we can do this, then what we eat might set the story of humanity on a path toward better days.

NOTES

Translations of German sources provided by Ayça Türkoğlu.

1. Yuval Noah Harari, *Sapiens: A Brief History of Humankind* (New York: HarperCollins, 2015).

2. Athenaeus, *Deipnosophistae* 12.517–8, trans. C. B. Gulick (Cambridge, MA: Loeb Classical Library, 1928/1969).

3. D. H. Lawrence, *Etruscan Places* (New York: The Viking Press, 1932).

4. Jerónimo Lobo, *A Voyage to Abyssinia*, trans. Samuel Johnson (New York: Cassel & Company, 1887).

5. E. A. de Cosson, *The Cradle of the Blue Nile: A Visit to the Court of King John of Ethiopia* (London: John Murray 1877).

6. Anthimus, *Anthimus: On the Observance of Foods*, trans. Mark Grant (London: Prospect Books, 2007).

7. Petra Hirscher, *Heilen und Kochen mit Hildegard von Bingen* (Stuttgart: TRIAS Verlag, 2010).

8. Alvise Cornaro, *Vom maßvollen Leben oder die Kunst gesund alt zu werden* (Berlin: Regenbrecht Verlag, 2022).

9. Robert Gugutzer, "Körperkult und Schönheitswahn. Wider den Zeitgeist," *Politik und Zeitgeschichte* 18 (2007): 4.

10. Heinrich Hoffmann, *Slovenly Peter der Struwwelpeter, or, Happy Tales and Funny Pictures*, trans. Mark Twain (New York: Harper & Brothers, 1935).

11. *Koch und Kellermeisterei* (Frankfurt: Gedruckt, 1556); see mori.bz.it/gastronomia/Kock=%20und%20Kellermeister.pdf.

12. Stefan Scholl, "Borschtsch soll Welterbe werden. Russland und Ukraine streiten um Rote-Bete-Suppe" ("Borscht should be granted world heritage status: Russia and Ukraine fight over beetroot soup"), *Lindauer Zeitung*, November 2020.

13. Press conference by the Russian foreign minister, April 8, 2022.

14. UNESCO: Intangible Cultural Heritage, "Culture of Ukrainian Borscht Cooking," ich.unesco.org/en/USL/culture-of-ukrainian-borscht-cooking-01852. Accessed February 20, 2024.

15. UNESCO: Intangible Cultural Heritage, "Browse the Lists of Intangible Cultural Heritage and the Register of good safeguarding practices," ich.unesco.org/en/USL/culture-of-ukrainian-borscht-cooking-0185%202. Accessed February 20, 2024.

16. Georg Philipp Harsdörffer, *Vollständiges und von neuem vermehrtes Trincir-Buch* (Nuremberg: Gerhard Fürst, 1657); see digital.slub-dresden.de/werkansicht/dlf/17244/1.

17. Massimo Montanari, *Der Hunger und der Überfluß: Kulturgeschichte der Ernährung in Europa* (Munich: Verlag C. H. Beck, 1993).

18. Julia Child, *Mastering the Art of French Cooking* (New York: Alfred A. Knopf, 1961/1970).

19. Wolfram Siebeck, *Kochschule für Anspruchsvolle* (Munich: Nymphenburger, 1976).

20. Eduard von Keyserling, "Zur Psychologie des Komforts," *Feiertagsgeschichten* (Göttingen: Steidl Verlag, 2008).

21. Ibid.

22. Joachim Nettelbeck, *Des Seefahrers Joachim Nettelbeck höchst erstaunliche Lebensgeschichte von ihm selbst erzählt* (Göppingen: Herwig, 1994; originally published 1821).

23. Antonia Maria Humm et al., eds., *König & Kartoffel: Friedrich der Große und die preußischen "Tartuffoli"* (Berlin: Verlag für Berlin-Brandenburg, 2012).

24. Ibid.

25. Hedwig Heyl, *Das ABC der Küche* (Berlin: Berlin Habel, 1897); see archive.org/details/bub_gb_09QqAAAAYAAJ.

26. George Kennan, *Siberia and the Exile System, Vol. 2* (New York: The Century Co., 1891).

27. Christian Kassung Fleisch, *Die Geschichte einer Industrialisierung* (Paderborn: Ferdinand Schöningh, 2020).

28. Alfred Polgar, "Theorie des 'Cafe Central,'" *Kleine Schriften* 4 (1926): 254–59.

29. Peter Altenberg, *Telegrams of the Soul: Selected Prose of Peter Altenberg*, trans. Peter Wortsman (New York: Archipelago Books, 2005).

30. *Die alte Mensa am Wilhelmsplatz: Geschichtsträchtiges Tagungshaus* (Göttingen: Georg-August-Universität, 2016).

31. Judith Hecht, "Pablo Picasso: Even a Cooking Pot Can Scream," *Falstaff* magazine, July 21, 2022, falstaff.com/en/news/pablo-picasso-even-a-cooking-pot-can-scream.

32. Alice B. Toklas, *The Alice B. Toklas Cook Book* (New York: Harper & Brothers, 1954).

33. Andrew Lam, "The Marvel of Bánh Mì," *The Cairo Review of Global Affairs* 18 (2015).

34. Ibid.

35. Yang Jisheng, *Grabstein – Mùbei: Die große chinesische Hungerkatastrophe 1958–1962* (Frankfurt: S. Fischer Verlag, 2012).

36. *Kalte Küche von A–Z* (Hamburg: Essen & Trinken, 1977).

37. Louis Fritzsche, *Illustrierte Tafelkultur* (Holzminden: Volker Hennig Verlagsbuchhandlung, 2000; originally published 1918).

ABOUT THE AUTHOR

UTA SEEBURG earned a PhD in literary studies and worked for many years as an editor at the German edition of *Architectural Digest*. There, she reported on design and travel and wrote numerous culinary essays. She now devotes herself entirely to writing books.